FISHING TACKLE
MAKING, MAINTENANCE AND IMPROVEMENT

Fishing Tackle

Making, Maintenance and Improvement

Barrie Rickards

and

Ken Whitehead

With contributions from
Les Beecroft

Adam and Charles Black
London

First published 1981
A & C Black (Publishers) Ltd
35 Bedford Row, London WC1R 4JH

ISBN 0 7136 2054 4

Rickards, Barrie
  Fishing tackle.
  1. Fishing tackle
  I. Title   II. Whitehead, Kenneth E
  688.7'9   SH447

  ISBN 0-7136-2054-4

Filmset by August Filmsetting, Reddish, Stockport

Printed in Great Britain by
Hollen Street Press Ltd, Slough, Berks

Contents

Introduction

The making and maintenance of fishing tackle, the improvement of design features and the constant development of new ideas, is a vast field we could never hope to cover in the form of a manufacturer's manual. But though we are not particularly accomplished as craftsmen, we are both inventive and capable of making praçtical products which, in some cases, are better than those of the commercial manufacturer – at least in terms of design if not of finish. We think that our rod rests, for example, are better than anything on the market, and we have more advanced ideas on these, as yet untried, that we have no space to include here. This book, therefore, is about what the average handyman angler can make and what he can repair. What he makes will certainly be cheaper and probably better than the commercial article – always assuming one exists. Our 'average handyman angler' by the way, is one who wishes to spend most of his spare time at the waterside, and least in the workshop. We do not assume the skills required for machine tool making, the use of lathes, or the experience of metalcraft necessary for the making of hooks. We do not expect our average angler to make fishing reels or fishing baskets: we *do* expect him to tie flies and to make and repair rods.

   The kinds of tools we envisage being available are those we have ourselves: electric drills or hand drills, saws, knives, a vice, a workbench, files and rasps, paints and brushes, varnishes and glues. Since so many people (probably rightly) regard anglers as being a bit soft in the head, we have never experienced any difficulty in obtaining expert help with things like welding, or the use of a lathe. To the pathetically helpless, experts enjoy exhibiting their skills. The little woman with the punctured tyre has known this for years.

1 BASIC TOOLS. Where others are needed they are mentioned in the text. Rasp to left; fine and 10 in. bastard file to right.

Among other matters we have excluded the making of boats and camping equipment: whilst our boating and camping is specifically geared to fishing we feel that these activities are strictly peripheral. However, though we do relatively little sea fishing nowadays, much that is written here is applicable to that sphere of the sport. Nevertheless, we have made plenty of sea fishing knick-knacks over the years and may well write about some of these at some future time.

For the present, we have planned this volume in three parts. In Part One we deal with the basic items – rods, reels, floats, leads, etc: Part Two is devoted to miscellaneous tackle (some would say this is the most important!), and Part Three encompasses what might broadly be termed game fishing, plus spinning. We have, in all cases, deliberately picked items which give a good spread of tackle-making techniques as well as, we hope, a lot of fundamentally useful gear. Nevertheless, we are always ready to welcome new ideas and to hear from readers who may feel that some specific has been unjustly omitted.

Finally, a word to our many good friends in the tackle trade. We have had good cause to be grateful to you on many occasions and we hope that this volume – which, after all, incites anglers to make, not buy – is not taken amiss. We hope you will console yourselves with the knowledge that any book which increases interest in our sport must, in the end, be good for business.

BARRIE RICKARDS
4 Willow Crescent, Milton, Nr Cambridge

KEN WHITEHEAD
Bwlchagored Farmhouse,
Llangadog, Dyfed

PART ONE

Rods, reels, floats and leads

Rods

ROD-MAKING MATERIALS

Before discussing rod making and repairing it is necessary to study the various materials that are available in today's tackle world. Materials in the plural may come as a surprise to many anglers who have used only glass fibre, but before that particular substance flooded the angling market there were various woods used in the construction of rods, and many of those old timber items are still in use and giving sterling service to their owners today.

Occasionally they appear on the second-hand market (a subject that is later given a section of its own) and provided that the purchaser knows what he is looking at, and what his requirements are, they may represent a fair purchase. But note that we are not discussing or considering such rods as antiques, or advocating purchase as a financial investment; there *is* a growing investor's market for these items, but this book is devoted to the practical aspects of tackle production.

GREENHEART

This was one of the most popular of all angling timbers and used for the construction of just about any type of rod imaginable from the humble single-handed spinning rod to the massive 18 ft spliced salmon fly rod. Even after the introduction and acceptance of split cane as the supreme material for wooden rods, greenheart was still used for cheaper items, especially where weight was not of great importance. It continued in use as a material for top joints in the cheaper rod ranges up to, and just after the last war, usually in combination with whole cane for the butt and/or middle joint sections.

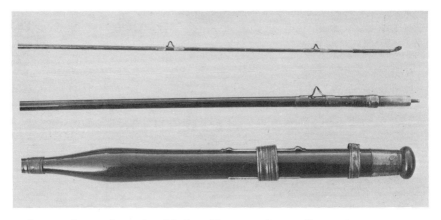

2 A greenheart fly rod, with handle turned out of one piece.

In appearance the wood is close-grained, moderately hard, and in its natural and unfinished state a very light straw colour. During the production stages it is usually stained and varnished, when it assumes a dark mahogany brown colour. If well seasoned it is reasonably resistant to warping and not given to excessive shrinking, but this is no guarantee that it will not suddenly, and without any warning, snap clean in half.

Unfortunately, when this occurs the snap is frequently like the breaking of a carrot, leaving two blunt ends, unlike the more usual long splinter-type break that lends itself to easy repair. This very weakness has driven a large number of rods – especially in the fly range – into the dustbin over the years. But as a rod-building material it is worth considering especially where a very sweet, soft action is required without the need to punch long lines over long distances. In fact, there is at least one rod manufacturing company that is still turning out just this type of rod; there may be more.

At one time the snapping propensities of greenheart was attributed to a rapid 'drying-out' which could occur during the first one or two seasons of use. The suggested prevention for this was to strip all sections bare, then stand them in a tube (plastic down-piping from roof guttering would be a good modern material) plugged at one end and filled with raw linseed oil. After two or three months the sections were removed, allowed to dry, and the rod made up with its fittings again.

This oil treatment can certainly do no harm, and is especially useful for rods turned with the handle in one piece. The wooden handle is allowed to soak in oil in the same way as the other joints, the winch fittings etc. being added or replaced after the drying out period. If it is thought that a wooden handle is cold to the touch or too antiquated for the modern user, then it can be leather-wrapped, which makes it a warm and viable proposition.

LANCEWOOD

This coarse-grained wood is harder than greenheart, but is more likely to take a permanent bend through constant pressure. The pronounced grain ensures that any breaks are usually 'splinters'; long rents that can be glued and whipped to restore some semblance of the original shape and strength. Good quality lancewood is split from the whole piece before being turned into shape on the lathe, and was most often employed for top joints in coarse fishing rods, with any permutation of wood being used as butt and middle joints, especially cane, greenheart, Spanish reed etc.

We can best describe lancewood as a useful timber and one that repairs easily, but lacks the 'feel' and straightness of greenheart, to which it is a second best.

3 Whole cane (top) and lancewood (below). The cane shows a good smooth node from which little will have to be removed when making a whole cane rod piece. A lumpy node, if removed, seriously weakens the piece.

MISCELLANEOUS TIMBERS

Rather an odd heading, but to complete the hardwood section one must consider some of the odds and ends that crop up from time to time. Quite a few timbers have been employed in rod building – in fact, for some years Ken fished with a four-section coarse rod turned out of beech; reasonably hard-wearing, but with no give or play, so that he often had the impression that he was fishing with a poker. Still, with finances as they were in those days . . .

Hickory has been used – and abused – for a large number of years and by an even larger number of sea anglers who have found in it an ideal medium for boat rods, although the wood tends to take a slow set after a prolonged period of really heavy use.

One-piece ash rods often 14 ft or more in length were commonplace at one time, especially in the North of England, where they were used for sea fishing off the rocks and beaches. Great stuff in use and certainly long lasting, but very heavy where handholding was the order of the day. Like hickory and beech, ash was only used for heavy rods and these would rarely split or snap. The rods that do turn up today are capable of being adapted to modern accessories such as leather handles, reinforced ferrules, Diamite rings, etc., and are well worth consideration by the angler.

For a short time after the last war when angling materials were in short supply quite a large number of billiard cues were turned into boat rods for sea work, and Ken knows several anglers on the south coast who still use them.

They are still capable of being adapted by whipping a Fuji Micas reel fitting approximately 18 in. above the butt end, wrapping leather hand-grips above and below it, and whipping on four or more rod rings (dependant on the length of cue) and a suitable tip ring. The whole job takes about an evening to do and provided that some careful varnishing is given to the whole rod, then the results will last a lifetime. Clumsy though these rods may sound they will take a fair amount of punishment where really hard work such as conger fishing over rocks is indulged in. An added advantage is that should the whole thing part company or disappear overboard then the owner has suffered little financial loss!

WHOLE CANE

The search for lightness in rod building led to the use of cane as a rod material. Most varieties have been used at some time or other, principally for the butt and middle joints of cheaper rods – and not only in the coarse fishing range. A large number of sea rods such as Burma Poles, and some fly rods, have been built with the whole cane lower sections, many of which have retained their strength and feel through the years.

The most popular cane has been Chinese Tonkin, a hard-skinned, round, tapering variety, dark brown in colour with lighter mottled patches and very evenly placed nodes. Next in the hard varieties is Brazilian cane, a darker, heavier wood with uneven nodes that are thick, rather ugly but very strong. It was especially popular as the material for 12–14 ft beach casters just after the last war and many of these rods have survived. Providing that the wood was not over-heated when the baking and straightening process was applied in the early production stages, or that too much wood was not stripped from the nodes in an attempt to lighten the joints, then these rods will give a lifetime of work, requiring nothing more than a coat of varnish every other season or so.

The real lightness in the various selections of cane is contained in Spanish and Japanese reed, each originating from the respective countries. Imported with match fishing in mind, they made excellent rods but few of them have survived into today's world. They are light yellow in colour, thin-skinned, fragile and given to depressed fractures if they are squashed, such fractures being very difficult if not impossible to repair. Often the wood at the nodes was sanded down in an effort to lose weight to such an extent that the joint itself was weakened, so a sudden heavy strain could cause a fracture even during a normal strike at a fish.

To strengthen the weakened areas massive whippings, often involving several hundreds of yards of silk, served their purpose until the covering varnish cracked. Water seeping under the silk hastened the rods' breakdown by rotting. So, by and large, these lightweight canes are best left alone, or placed in the hands of an antique collector.

SPLIT CANE OR BUILT CANE

A rod material that needs little introduction or description, most anglers being familiar with the hexagonal strips that are machined and then glued together to form the tapered, fine-actioned rods that have been designed for every style of fishing. Nevertheless, a few words here on the characteristics and faults of built cane may help the angler who is offered a ready-made rod, or thinking of constructing one for himself.

Good quality split cane is medium yellow in colour, and has a smooth, even surface. A dark yellow appearance is often an indication that the cane has been overheated in the curing process of the raw cane, whilst a white appearance indicates that the outer dermis, or skin, has been heavily machined. Both are faults that may let both rod and angler down. The various strips, when glued together, should meet perfectly, and not show gaps. Early rods were fixed with animal glue, which over the years tended to break down, allowing the strips to part and let in water – a fault that literally knocks all the stuffing out of a rod's casting ability. Some rods were made with a steel centre. In effect this was a length of steel wire running through the centre of the hexagonal strips, and was intended to impart strength and spring. Though effective in the rod's infancy, there are few that have not given way to internal rusting with age, making yet another problem for the unwary user to cope with.

The strength of split cane lies in its outer surface or skin; top joints, by virtue of their fine tolerances, have little of this skin available to supply firmness. Unless the cane used in their construction was properly cured and set together, then there is every risk that it will become 'soft' or take a bend into whichever direction the joint is most curved. Once this happens (and it is a frequent occurrence with fly rods) there is not much in the way of guts left to punch the line out during a cast, or to drive the hook home on the strike.

The other major drawback to split cane lies in its tendency to take a 'set', or permanent curve. This invariably happens when the rod has been stood on end, against a wall or in a corner, and not hung by the loop provided in the end of the rod bag. There is a cure for this – by removing the rod rings and fittings and then re-whipping them with the set, or curve, uppermost, so that future use will return the timber to its original shape. A labour, but one of love if that is the sole fault to be found in the timber.

From this long list of possible faults the reader will no doubt have gathered that split cane is temperamental, and not a material to consider in a rod unless it is comparatively new, or unless the owner is willing to take both time and trouble to maintain it, a subject that will be discussed later. There is a lot of old cane about (at a price) and providing that it is sound, it is a sensible investment. But beware – check thoroughly before deciding that the particular rod you are offered will be either worth the money that is asked, or able to perform the duties that you have in mind.

Any angler who would attempt making his own split cane, assuming he can obtain good quality whole cane to split, should try reading a famous book, *Rod Building for Amateurs* by Richard Walker. Although out of print it may yet be available in libraries. In this book Walker explains how to make each of the (usually) six strips, and, indeed, once built a machine that would actually cut the strips! He also goes into the construction of hollow built cane, double-built cane, flat strip cane and other constructions. In this day and age these are, sadly, things to be made by the highly-skilled fanatic and are hence rather out of the scope of this volume.

FIBRE GLASS

In the late 1950s Richard Walker was able to write, truthfully, that built cane would do anything that steel or the relatively new fibre glass could do. How things have changed! Steel is now almost non-existent in rod making (though Barrie has a 12 ft bottom rod still in serviceable condition) whilst glass has improved beyond recognition. Only in the late 1970s has it had to face up to a competitor in carbon fibre.

Early fibre glass was dreadful and was mostly seen as solid (blue/green) glass in short spinning rods or boat rods. We knew a man who suffered the indignity of his end piece disintegrating into a mess like glass wool as the fibres came apart! As the resins and the contained fibres improved, hollow glass came into use, and a real improvement it was, enabling longer, lighter rods to be made. However, in the early years little effort was made to control the wall thickness (they were mostly parallel-wall even to the tip, where they became more or less solid) and some rather ugly rods, by modern standards, resulted: discerning anglers at the time stayed with split cane until manufacturers began building glass blanks with tapered walls.

This brings us to modern glass. Several firms make a fine glass cloth, in which it is difficult with the naked eye to see the fabric pattern. The mandrels (which control overall shape and taper) are wrapped with great care and the cloth bonded with high quality resins. The amount of glass cloth wrapped at any one point determines the thickness of the wall, and this and the overall taper controls the rod action – be it fast or slow. A steep taper increases the speed, as does decreased overall wall thickness and increased wall taper from butt region to tip.

None of these matters need worry the D.I.Y. angler too much for he will be buying his blanks ready-made, with or without spigots attached. It *is* possible to make your own blanks, but as with reel making and split cane making it is a task generally beyond the scope of even the most enthusiastic fisherman. Deciding on which blank is really a question dealt with by Les Beecroft, when he discusses the building of a good rod of various types (see page 31). Naturally, you have to decide what *type* of rod you want, what *length* it shall be, whether it shall be fast or slow taper, and perhaps what overall weight. You then seek the advice of one or more tackle dealers, examine plenty of blanks or, better still, try rods already made up of those blanks and compare them. Having decided on a blank you can usually then decide to buy them with the spigots fitted or not. The particular blanks in wide use include Fibatube, Conoflex, North Western, Sportex and Marco – all are excellent in their different ways.

CARBON FIBRE

There is always considerable resistance to the arrival of new materials, in this case caused partially by poor resin bonding initially (shades of fibre glass!) and by high costs. The former problem has disappeared entirely and a whole range of carbon fibre rods and unmade-up blanks are available to the angler: roach poles, long match rods, fly rods, even pike rods. High costs, or relatively high costs, are likely to remain for some years, for carbon fibre is a by-product of the aerospace industry and angling takes only a tiny proportion of the product. Until such time as large-scale replacement of certain metals takes place in the aerospace industry costs to the angler will remain high.

Most rod materials, past and present, comprise fibres bonded either naturally (as in cane) or artificially (as in glass) and carbon fibre is no exception. As a generalisation carbon fibres are finer and stiffer than glass, and stronger, so that when used in the right proportions with correct resins they produce a tube which is lighter than glass for the same strength. The rods produced to do the same job as glass tend to be thinner, so that they cut or can be pushed through the air more easily; they are lighter (therefore less fatiguing) and they are stiffer. This last word needs a little explanation: in a sense the rod is faster, and there is less wobble or vibration on recovery from a swing whether this is on the cast or the strike. The whole action is lighter, easier, and sweeter to use, although at first you do feel as if you are using a fragile wand for heavy work, whether this latter is throwing a fly line or playing a big fish.

Almost all modern anglers are agreed that carbon fibre blanks are better than glass, but they are as yet much more expensive. However, the two materials, hollow glass and carbon fibre, give to the modern angler two superb materials far better than anything available in the past: split cane is beautiful to look at and to use, and Barrie still has several rods of this material, but it *is* heavier and it *is* more prone to damage.

METAL FERRULES

If we have given the impression thus far that all new things are welcomed with open arms, this certainly does not apply in the case of metal ferrules versus spigots. Metal ferrules certainly stiffen up the rod action a little and they are heavier and more clumsy looking (particularly reinforced ones), but they *are* strong. In general, glass spigots do all that is required of them, but for the real hard work involved in casting heavy weights they seem to crack more commonly than do metal ferrules. In fact, only once have either of us seen a metal ferrule collapse.

But with the wide acceptance of hollow glass rods, and the

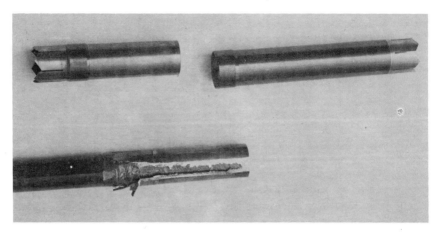

4 Difficult and careful removal of male ferrule partly completed on split cane rod: replacement ferrules shown in appropriate position.

ease to manufacturers of fitting spigots, metal ferrules have become less common on rods and less readily available to the amateur rod builder. Indeed, they are fast disappearing from the tackle catalogues.

Fitting metal ferrules has really only one difficult stage, namely that of deciding on the size for the junction you wish to make. Whether the ferrule is being fitted to glass (or carbon) or cane, it is a great mistake to remove glass or cane to make a fit. Try to pick a size that is a tightish fit or a loose fit: you can build up to the latter. When fitting metal ferrules to glass it is a good idea to *gently* rough up the glass surface with fine sandpaper and to glue part of both male and female ferrules to the glass. When fitting to cane this is not really necessary.

If the ferrule is to be fitted to split cane it may be necessary to round off the cane where it is to go under the ferrule by glueing on thin slivers of cane to the flats. After glueing it is always necessary to sand them down so that the overall cross section is round and makes a smooth fit into the ferrule. However, we have found that equally commonly the serrated ends of the ferrules sit neatly on the cane flats (and the angles of the hexagon on the inside walls of the ferrule), and building up on the flats is not necessary provided the serrated ends are well glued down and whipped.

If the ferrules form a good, tight, push-fit on the cane or glass, then it is only necessary to smear the surfaces with Araldite and to push home the ferrule, wipe off the extruded Araldite, and whip over the top of the serrated part of the ferrule and about half an inch up the full tube part (Photo. 6). Before glueing, make sure that when the male ferrule is in the female ferrule the gap between the two ends of the blanks is only a few millimetres: gaps of half an inch or more cause a weak junction. This position, prior to glueing, can be made certain by marking the cane or glass with a pencil at the point the serrated ends should reach. When glueing, the ferrules are pushed on to this mark.

If the glass or cane needs building up it is best to do this with fine thread and to get this thoroughly tested before smearing glue on the threaded region. Our experience is that we tend always to put on too much thread and have to take some off.

5 From the top: reinforced metal ferrules with overlapping binding silk; solid spigot on lightweight spinning rod, showing correct gap between rod parts, but lacking whipping near shoulder of male part and neck of female part; hollow glass spigot, gap too wide; hollow glass spigot, not seen because gap dangerously close.

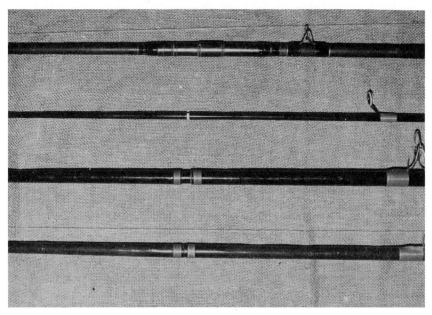

Having obtained a good push-fit, during which testing the threads become a little worn and flattened, it is only necessary to glue as already described. Finally, whip over the serrated part of the ferrule, and a little way over the tubed part, exactly as before. The procedure for whipping is described on pages 28–30.

HOLLOW SPIGOTS

Hollow spigots should be about the same wall thickness, or *fractionally* more, than the rod pieces they are joining, and they should not be too long. On a 10 ft stepped-up carp rod the total spigot length would be around 6 in.; on a 14 ft Fibatube match rod, perhaps 7–8 in. The best way to obtain the right spigot is to buy it at the time you buy the blank. As stated earlier, the tackle dealer may well fit it for you. But if you prefer to do it yourself proceed as follows.

First, cut the blank or have it cut at the exact point you wish to make the join. Make a clean simple cut, with a small hacksaw, exactly at right-angles to the length of the rod. You can assist accuracy here by making a tape ring around the rod and checking that this is true before sawing along the side of it.

Then push the spigot into the top joint (or upper joint) but not so hard that it jams; glue has to go in there as well as glass! When it is in position mark the spigot with a pencil. Remove the spigot and drop it into the butt end of the butt piece (or lower piece) so that it pops out loosely at the junction. Pull it firmly into position and then mark this position also. The distance between the two marks should be about 5 mm, in other words rather farther apart than the gap at a well-fitted metal ferrule. During use the gap will wear smaller and it will be necessary to saw off short pieces from the upper piece, 2 mm at a time, to retain the best fit: several seasons should pass before it is necessary to do this.

Araldite is wiped into the inside of the upper end of the butt piece along the length where the spigot will lie. The spigot is then dropped into the butt end of the butt or lower piece *ensuring that it is the right way round*. The spigot usually appears without trouble and can be pulled into position, perhaps using a slight

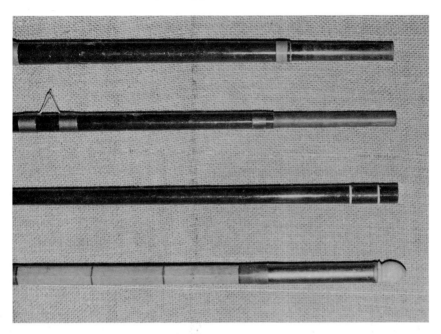

6 From the top: hollow glass spigot, shoulder whipping correct; hollow glass spigot, whipping too far from shoulder but of correct length; female part of join, whipping too far from neck; split cane butt piece, metal ferrule, overlapping whipping in correct position.

twisting motion if necessary. Remove the excess glue carefully: too much glue remaining on the male part will spoil the fit into the top or upper piece. The fitted ends of the two parts of the rod are then whipped from about 2 mm from the end to a distance of 8–10 mm from the end. This helps prevent splitting of the ends of the blanks.

It must be clear from the above that the choice of spigot size is very critical, and it is best to use the judgment of your tackle dealer for this. If you have to do it yourself you need quite a length of blank! First, drop it down the butt end of your intended rod blank until it just stops (it is unusual for things to jam at this stage). Mark the position on the rod blank where you intend cutting it; then measure from the butt end of the spigot blank to the desired amount of overlap making, on removal of the spigot blanks, two marks, one at the top of the intended spigot, the other at the bottom. Then, with your heart in your mouth, cut the spigot blank at the two marks. Obviously it is better to get a dealer to do this job, and the degree of accuracy required does explain the price of spigots on occasions.

SOLID SPIGOTS

The practice of using solid spigots appears to be increasing, both Intrepid and East Anglian Rod Co., for example, using them regularly. The material commonly used is polypropylene rod, and it must be said that the amateur will have some difficulty obtaining it for his own rod building in the desired tapers. Most are custom prepared for commercially designed rods. These

7 From the top: solid glass spinning rod, very basic, cheap metal ferrule, with incorrect ferrule whipping; cork handle with shaped shoulder; second blank same as first but with 'spinning ring' classically whipped; third rod with High Bells Life ring *side-whipped* to slender blank; fourth blank with solid spigot and single leg Fuji ring; last, a hollow glass blank with correct neck whipping.

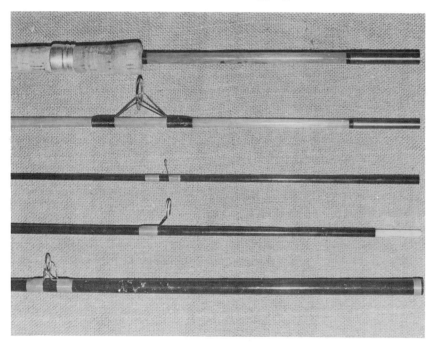

spigots are certainly strong, though whether they have any advantages over hollow ones is open to question. It should be noted that they do not necessarily stiffen the rod action: this result depends as much on the choice of spigot material as on its length. Fitting the spigot is exactly the same as for hollow spigots.

GLUES

Araldite in various drying speeds, or similar brands of epoxy resins, are almost universally used by tackle makers. When warmed Araldite can be run into the most obscure cracks and crannies and it is undoubtedly one of the best glues, particularly as it has a fairish filling ability, retaining its strength. Certainly for fitting spigots we would consider no other type. When fitting metal ferrules, however, such a powerful glue may not be necessary or desirable and one of the modern or old-fashioned wood glues will suffice. For cork handles too, we find Araldite too strong when it comes to repair time.

When you remember that the corks themselves take a firm grip then it is clear that the Bostick range is very suitable, and when corks need to be removed at a later stage it is so much easier to work. Durafix is a useful glue with which to coat whippings prior to varnishing: it prevents the varnish soaking into the whippings and thus changing the colour. One of the latest strong glues, Superglue, has its uses but it must be remembered that it is not a good filler and needs two clean, well-fitting surfaces for a good bond – which can sometimes be inconveniently immediate! Most D.I.Y. enthusiasts accumulate a wide variety of glues and fillers, and we are no exceptions. It is an acceptable extravagance.

ROD HANDLES

Home-made handles come in a variety of shapes and sizes, but gone are the days of wood (unless you like playing history) whilst modern composition handles (such as Intrepids) are at present in the commercial field only. Open to the amateur to choose from are, in order of popularity: cork rings; rubber or plastic grips; sheet cork; cord, and leather. It often seems to us that leather strip (and sometimes plastic tape) are added to the handles of fast taper blanks simply for aesthetic reasons or to give the angler reassurance that the rod has a handle! Cord handles are obviously of more use in that they provide a good grip which, as any beach fisherman will tell you, is a help under some conditions. All these materials are simply wound on a good impact adhesive and the ends carefully trimmed and protected by whipping in strong thread. They are often a delight to use and certainly relatively quick to prepare.

Two handles about which we have grave reservations, having tried them extensively, are sheet cork and rubber or plastic grips. Sheet cork is often used to give a nice feel or grip to a blank that is too thick to take anything other than an unsightly,

8 From the top: handle with simple sliding winch fittings and aesthetically shaped shoulder; second with Fuji reel clamp which, ideally, should have a thin layer of cork beneath it; screw winch fitting and plastic shoulder collar over ferrule.

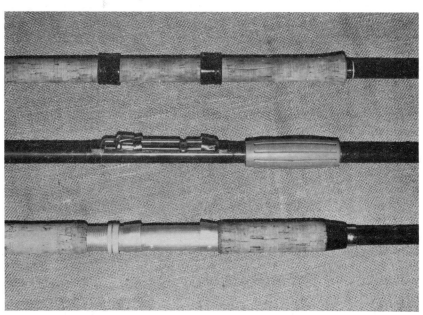

thick ring cork handle. If ring corks have to be shaved down very thin this presumably raised the question: why not use sheet cork? Why use cork at all, enquire our questioning minds. In such circumstances a handle comprising an untreated blank, Fuji fittings, or perhaps a cord or leather covering is far better.

However, should you wish to try sheet cork it is necessary to put a thin layer of impact adhesive carefully over the whole of one side of the cork sheet and then allow it to dry. Do the same with the rod blank, taking care not to put on too much, or to spread it too far along the blank. The blank is then rolled in the sheet cork to the extent that the cork begins to overlap itself. The tricky bit is trimming back the surplus cork, and this is done by first lifting the corner to see where the edge is, and then using this as a guide before cutting off the surplus with a Stanley knife. Should any gaps be left between the two cork edges they can be filled with a mixture of cork dust and Durafix, and then sanded down lightly with the finest sandpaper. Repairs to sheet cork handles, unfortunately frequently necessary, can be made in the same fashion after cutting away the tattered portion as neatly as possible.

The trouble with paired rubber grips is that only the one at the butt end serves any purpose; that is either for gripping with the left hand during casting or for protecting that end of the blank. The upper grip is *never* gripped because the right hand is on the reel seating on a fixed spool reel. With a centrepin or multiplier the right hand will be just *below* the reel, so the grip should be in this position if it is to be of any use.

Very careful measurement and trial is needed to get a pair that will fit your blank. Then it is necessary to cut off, with a Stanley knife, the blocked end of one of the grips so that it can be slid along the blank to the correct position. (Open-ended rubbers are also available.) This is done by starting at the *narrow* end of the blanks naturally! Soap solution may be needed to ease the grip to its position or, alternatively, one can be chosen that is slightly too loose and it can then be built up with thread and glue as explained earlier. The butt grip is simply pushed into position over a *little* glue, which latter is added to the blank when the grip only has about an inch to go.

But ring cork handles, glued and filed down to the required diameter, are still the most widely used rod handles. They are

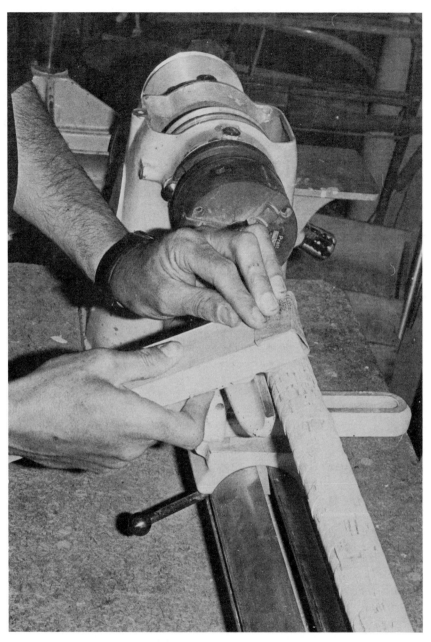

9 Shaping handle with glasspaper and block in wood lathe.

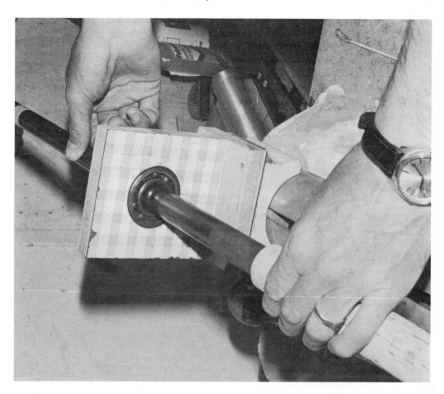

10 Les Beecroft's special ball-bearing adapter for holding the glass blank during handle turning on a wood lathe.

long-lasting, pleasant, and can be cleaned to near new with warm water and soap. Handle corks have different internal diameters and you simply choose the most appropriate tight fit for your blank. If the grip is too tight, or the blank diameter unusual in some other respect, simply open up the internal diameter of each cork with a round file. It is surprising how quickly this can be achieved.

When preparing a cork handle add the butt and collar corks, at the bottom and top of the handle respectively, last of all. But the rest of the corks are simply pushed on quickly after smearing with a clear Bostick glue (which we prefer to epoxy resins since no great strength is required). It is essential to glue the corks to each other as well as to the blank itself. Constantly wipe off excess glue, add the corks one by one and then allow to dry. Reason suggests that it is sensible to wait until the next day

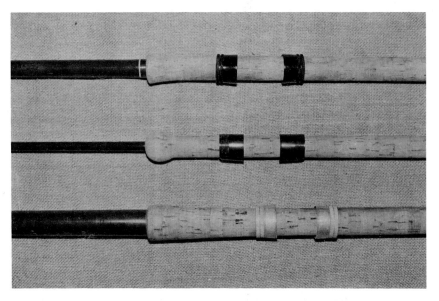

11 Different handle shoulders, each without a shoulder reinforcing collar.

before shaping, but we have often continued, impatiently, within the hour!

Decide on what diameter the handle should be, and its shape if it is to be anything but parallel-sided. Personally we prefer simple, parallel-sided, 1 in. diameter handles for our coarse fishing rods, both for comfortable grip and for aesthetic reasons. For the same reasons we prefer shaped corks at both butt and collar, rather than rubber buttons or metal collars.

The next step depends upon whether you are a real amateur, and in our league, or a professional, like Les Beecroft. We do our handle shaping by hand; the professional uses a lathe. Since lathes come in a great variety of types these days we will not attempt to explain their use, except to say that at wood-turning speed, and armed with various grades of sandpaper held *under* the turning handle-to-be, the angler can make a superbly finished job. A lot of judgment still has to be made by eye, but provided the work is done slowly and carefully there should be no problems.

By hand the job is more laborious but, in fact, we now do all our handles this way and produce a finish that is difficult to

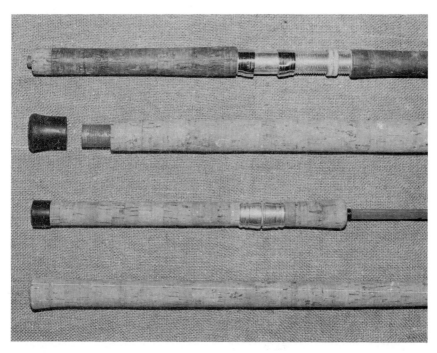

12 Different rod butts. Above, before fitting of plastic butt cap; below, with shaped cork end.

distinguish from the professional job. Hold the blank with its glued proto-handle away from you with the butt end (as yet unprotected by cork, remember) at a lower level, either on a bench or stool. Then with a rasp or a coarse 10 in. bastard file make long strokes down and away from you. Turn the handle a little with every stroke and try to operate uniformly along the length of the handle. One danger is that you may remove more material from those corks at the top and bottom than from those in the middle, so it pays to neglect attention to the ends since these can be brought into line later. It takes about half an hour to work a rough handle down to near the diameter needed. As you approach the 1 in. diameter it pays to inspect frequently, looking for bumps or hard patches of cork.

At this stage abandon the file and use decreasing grades of sandpaper. The sandpaper should be worked quickly but *lightly*, creating quite a bit of dust which, as it settles and jumps about the cork, actually betrays high and low spots to the practiced

eye. Strokes with the paper should be long, except when a bump
is detected. The sandpaper can be wrapped round a sanding
block of cork, or indeed, around a file.

The diameter now is best checked by setting a Vernier gauge
and running it up and down the handle: set it fractionally *over*
the preferred diameter and try to get the whole handle parallel
with only a mm or so to go. It then becomes an easy task, wrapping the finest grade of sandpaper around the handle (dispensing
with the block), to remove the last of the thickness of cork.

The final stage is to add corks to the top and bottom of the
handle from which to shape the mushroom ends. This job should
be done slowly and carefully after glueing in position. At no
stage have we suggested removing cork with a sharp knife,
thought this is indeed practised by many expert rod makers:
we find it easier to judge with a rasp or file, than with a knife.

REEL AND HANDLE FITTINGS

Certain handle fittings are largely cosmetic; for example,
shoulder ferrules and butt buttons, though the latter have some
value for boat and pier rods where the butt could take considerable wear if it had no protection. Fitting them is so easy:
it is the last job you do on the handle before fitting the rod rings,
and it is only necessary to leave the butt and shoulder corks
more or less unfiled until you are ready to fit the butt button or
shoulder ferrule. When ready, use a fine file and fine sandpaper
and shape the corks slowly and carefully, testing regularly to
see that the items will be aligned correctly before glueing. It is
not too serious a matter if too much cork is removed provided
it is removed evenly, because the gap can be filled with thread
and glue, as when fitting metal ferrules to rod blanks. For
coarse fishing rods, fly rods, and some sea rods we would leave
out both butt buttons and shoulder ferrules.

Reel mountings are a different question entirely: they are very
necessary although we know a few experienced anglers who
always tape their reels to the rod. In fact this is probably the
best way, but most of us lesser mortals make do with *screw
fittings, Fuji fittings,* or *sliding winch fittings* (Photos. 8, 11, 14).

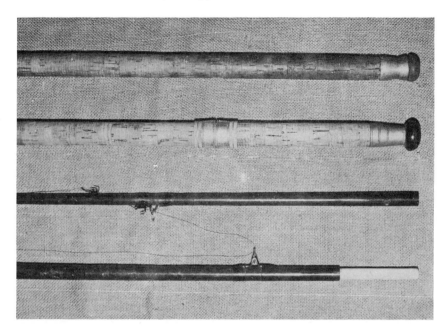

13 Above, rubber butt caps; below, heavy duty solid spigot, both male and female parts incorrect in that they lack shoulder and neck whippings.

The last are the easiest to fit. At a stage before the butt button is added and shaped, the rest of the handle has been reduced to its correct diameter (see previous section) and it is now that the correct size winch fittings should be chosen. Take care both to slide them on the handle the correct way round and to try your reels in position before committing yourself to doing the butt button or butt end cork. Nothing further is required.

Fuji fittings can be whipped to glass blanks or to cork or composition handles. When whipping direct to glass (many fast taper rods look unsightly with cork handles) it is a good idea to put a thin layer of cork between them and the glass because the base of the Fuji fitting may cut into the glass a little. Otherwise they can be whipped on using strong eye-tying thread or plaited nylon line.

Screw fittings are a little more difficult. Generally speaking they are seated on cork with a smaller diameter than the handle above and below the fitting (in other words, the rest of the handle

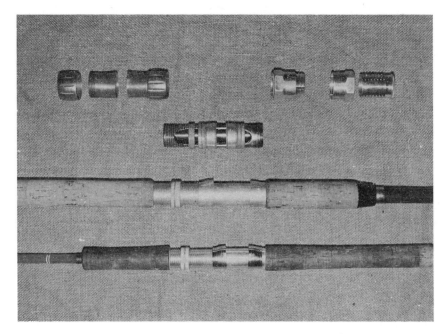

14 Various types of screw winch fittings, all the upper three sliding on handles which have *not* been indented in the manner of the lower two.

is thicker) so that the job must be done in two parts. First, one half of the handle should be corked, glued and shaped into position. Then the corks on which the screw fitting will sit are added, and filed down very carefully to the inside diameter of the latter. Again it is not too serious if too much cork is removed, but the sanding/filing down must be done evenly so that the fitting lies exactly parallel to the length of the rod. It can be glued in position in the usual way, and it is an advantage if a 5 mm gap is left between the corks which form the seating and those forming the handle, for this gap will take up surplus glue: the gap can be either left or cut carefully. Finally the other end of the handle is completed, and whether this is the top or the bottom depends only on which way round you constructed it. We prefer to do the top of the handle before the butt end.

ROD RINGS

These come in great variety but broadly can be divided into intermediate which stand well off the rod (High Bells Life) and those quite close to the rod (Low Bells Life, snake rings). Butt rings (the ring nearest the handle) can be the same and are more commonly lined with agate or a ceramic. End rings too can be low or stand off, and are usually similarly lined. All the rings can be lined, and for sea fishing some or all the rings might carry rollers. Whatever rings are chosen they should be the best you can afford – this is a case of buying, not making – preferably hard chrome of fine wire and as light as reasonable for the rod in use. The *best* unlined hard chrome rings do not groove.

The other critical factor in considering the rings is their spacing upon the rod: too many increase weight and soften the action of the rod; too few result in considerable friction since the line does not follow the curve of the rod during the playing of a fish (Fig. **A**). This in turn results in too much line wear, not to mention a certain difficulty in playing big fish. The ring spacings on several rods are recommended by Les Beecroft (page 38) so measurements are not given here, but suffice it to say that rings should not be placed too near the ferrules or

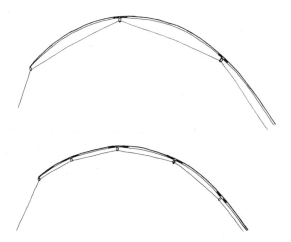

Fig. **A** Correctly ringed rod shown below. With the upper rod bent into an arc the ring spacing will cause great resistance.

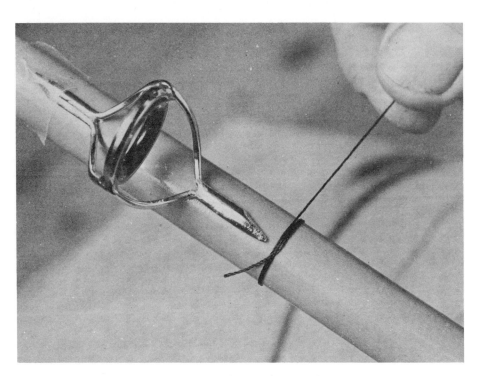

15–18 Stages in whipping on rod rings.

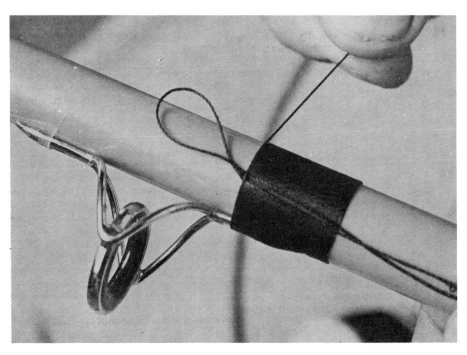

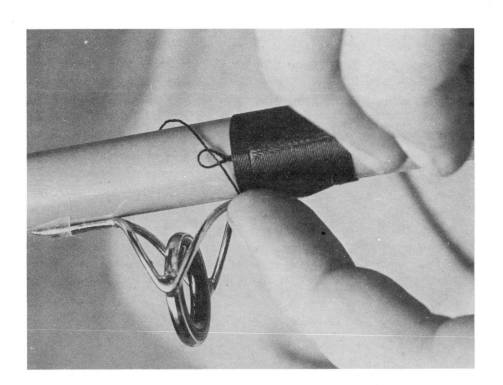

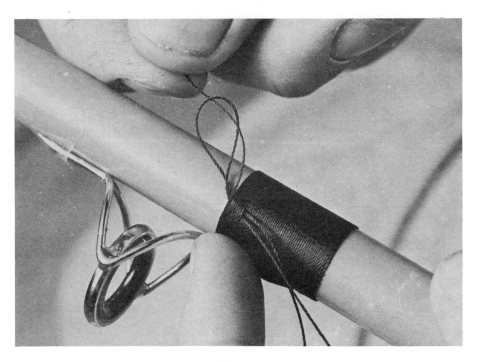

spigots or, indeed, too close to the top of the handle. One other consideration is necessary for the end or tip ring of coarse fishing rods, namely, whether or not to fit a ring which will take a swing or quiver tip. Since such rings are now common and of good quality, both stand off and low, we fit them as standard on all except our pike rods. Even a long rod can be pressed into swing tip service occasionally.

Whipping a ring in place is simplicity itself although it is one of the things which often amazes the newcomer to rod building, since at first he finds it a slow and arm-aching process. It goes without saying that the rings have been correctly spaced and lined up: there is no earthly reason why all the rings need not be sellotaped in position before any work is begun. Some anglers prefer to put on a first thin layer of varnish before putting on the rings and there is certainly some advantage, from a preservational point of view, with some rods. With glass rods we would never bother about it.

One leg of the ring is sellotaped down (Photo. 15) or, as we prefer to do it, *both* are sellotaped down, but with only a small amount of sellotape. We place this tape so that it forms a rise up on to the leg around which the tying silk can be tied without unsightly gaps appearing between the silk loops. With badly formed ring legs it may even be necessary to file them smooth before beginning the process.

Many rod makers hold the tying silk to the rod with the thumb of the left hand near the leg, before beginning winding with the right hand. We prefer to use a tiny triangle of sellotape to hold it or alternatively use the tape which is holding the leg in place. After this it is merely a matter of winding round the silk until it rides over, trapping its own end, then the ring leg, and on towards the ring itself. Before the upright parts of the legs are reached, just below the ring itself, it is necessary to bind in a 3 in. loop of the same or stronger thread to act as a pull-through as the whipping is completed.

This latter step is achieved, when the desired length of whipping has been added, by passing the end of the whipping thread through the loop, and then pulling the loop out backwards so that it disappears beneath the whipping. Keep pulling so that it comes altogether clear of the whipping and then trim off the length of whipping thread which projects.

VARNISHES

We admit to holding strong views on the subject of varnishes. Frankly, none of our hollow glass rods have any varnish except on the whippings, which first receive a coating of clear Durafix, sanding sealer or cellulose sealer. We are aware that glass can absorb some moisture but most of our rods have been going along quite happily for over a decade so the damage from this source can hardly be very serious. However, no form of cane can be treated like this and the wood must be varnished to keep out moisture.

We liked the old-fashioned shellac varnish which after a layer or two imparted a nice brown colour to the wood, the more so as the varnish aged. Today we use the same, or a modern varnish such as Copal, but always top off with a matt varnish of which there are several brands available. There is no place in fishing for high-gloss rods and we are happy to see that they are rapidly disappearing from the scene. We still feel that varnish is best applied with the fingers rather than with spray or brush, although the brush can be helpful in difficult corners. Using a finger, a very thin layer of varnish can be laid, allowed to dry, and then another thin layer added and so on. Several very thin layers are much more durable and flexible than a small number of thick layers, particularly on soft-action rods which often crack and flake the thick varnish layers seen on commercially produced rods.

We have always been strongly opposed to the painting of rods, much preferring the natural wood showing through varnish, but with glass rods this becomes less of an aesthetic requirement, and we have seen several sets of custom-built rods belonging to specimen hunters, and which have been painted dull, matt shades of green and brown. They are certainly attractive in a waterside setting.

BUILDING A SELECTION OF RODS

In our experience the first item of tackle an angler attempts to make for himself is a rod. In earlier pages we have itemised and discussed in detail the various operations in making a rod from scratch. Avoiding repetition, we have now selected a collection of rods to be made, using blanks as bought from your tackle shop. The spigots will be already fitted and all the fittings are available over the tackle shop counter.

TWELVE-FOOT FLOAT MATCH ROD

Several different makes of blanks are available for this rod and your main considerations should be the action required and the weight; each will vary in either aspect. To guide the newcomer selecting a blank for the first time the Fibatube range will give a good general purpose rod when finished. If you are looking for a very light, tip actioned rod then we would suggest you look at the Cono-flex range.

Having selected the blank, the fittings will be the next consideration. We will begin with the rings. The rings used on today's rods are usually either High Bells or the new Fuji three-legged rings. Speaking personally we have not found any outstanding advantage with the Fuji rings to justify the high price (slightly more than double). Our personal preference is to use hard chrome High Bells rings in size 0 all through, apart from the butt ring. By using size 0 rings the weight saving is quite considerable. One can then put extra rings on the rod to prevent line sticking to the rod in wet weather. On our own 12 ft match rods we have ten rings plus a butt ring. The spacings for these, in inches reading from the tip, are 4, 5, 6, 8, 9, 10, 12, 13, 14, 14.

Next, the handle corks. These can either be purchased in 6 in. bored lengths or as individual rings, and the length required can be calculated by taping your reel to the blank in the position you prefer to use it and holding the blank at this position. The base of the handle should now extend approx. 3–4 in. beyond (below) the elbow. The handle corks should extend above the reel position for 4–6 in.

The sundry fittings will include a reel fitting. This can either be the sliding rings or the Fuji strap fittings. Butt caps are seldom used these days, anglers preferring the corks to be rounded off at the base. Whipping nylon will be required in the colour of your choice. This can now be purchased in impregnated form, eliminating the need to dope the finished whipping to maintain its colour without stains.

With all our components assembled we can commence building our rod. We begin with the handle. The corks are glued on the bottom section of the blank over the position previously explained. Before glueing in place, rough up this section of the blank with a file or sandpaper to obtain a good glueing surface. When glueing corks in place do not forget to slip on the sliding reel fittings. Reference to the section on handles (page 17) will help you during this exercise.

With the handle fitted and sanded down to shape we are ready to start whipping on the rod rings. The rings are first prepared by filing down the ends of the legs to a feather edge and ensuring that the undersides of the ring feet are flat. Mark off on the blank the ring positions. Place rings in turn in position and using sellotape tape them, by one leg only, in position. Check the alignment of all rings on each section. Satisfied that the rings are positioned correctly, whip the untaped side of each ring working as detailed on pages 28–30. When all rings have one side whipped, remove the sellotape and repeat with the opposite sides. Fit tip ring to rod, again using the high, stand-off position. One last whipping job remains and that is to whip a length of approx. $\frac{3}{4}$ in. at the base of the top and middle joints, starting as close to the bottom as possible. Also, repeat these whippings at the top of the butt and middle sections, starting close to the point where the spigot protrudes.

The above, with reference to the earlier pages, should give you enough information to complete a satisfactory rod. Rod blanks can also be bought in 13 ft or 14 ft lengths. Should you be unable to find the correct action required in say a 13 ft or 14 ft blank, this can sometimes be obtained by buying a 12 ft blank and extending the butt section under the handle with a spare length of fibre glass or alloy tubing. This will give a butt section longer than the other two joints but this is of no disadvantage, particularly if the right action is obtained.

SWING TIP/QUIVER TIP ROD

The next rod in our selection is a rod suitable for using with a swing tip or quiver tip. With the fishing pressure on waters today fish have become increasingly more difficult to catch. This situation has made fishing with fine lines necessary to

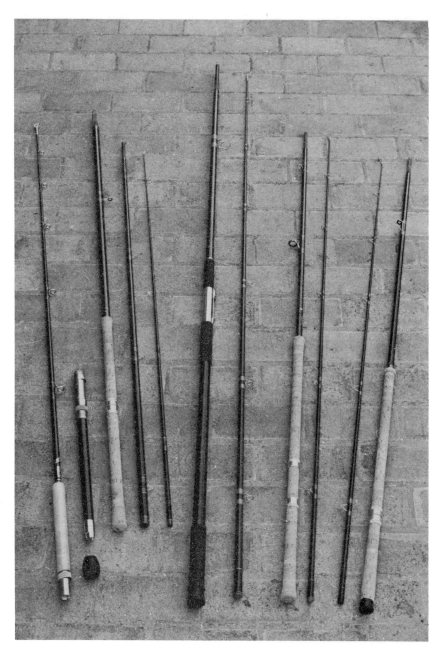

19 The rods built by Les Beecroft as a set of rods for this volume. From the left: boat rod; twelve-foot match rod; beachcaster; pike rod; carp rod.

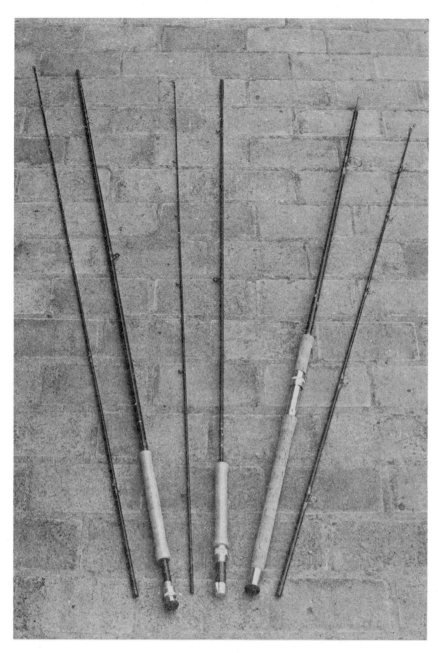

20 As Photo. 19. Continuing from the left: 9 ft 3 in. reservoir rod; carbon fibre rod; spinning rod. See text for full description of the rods in these two photographs.

ensure success. When fishing waters for large fish, e.g. bream, tench, etc. with these fine lines, e.g. 2–2½ lb b.s., a soft, tip-actioned rod is required, without the action coming too far down: about halfway would be an absolute maximum. This is the rod that we have in mind for this exercise.

Finding a blank marketed as a swing tip blank, with this kind of action, may present a problem. What we suggest you look at are the 9½ ft or 10 ft fly rod blanks. Blanks designed to take either size 8 or 10 fly lines are generally the range to look at. One that Les Beecroft uses for his own rods is the Cono-flex 9 ft 8 in. reservoir fly blank. This makes up into an ideal swing tip rod. With such a rod he has struck into bream at distance using 2 lb b.s. line and had no fear of breaking on the strike. Another blank of similar action is marketed by Modern Arms Co. (Marco) under the name of 'Hornet' fly rod. Both blanks are, of course, two-piece and are either matt black or brown in colour.

We make up the handle using corks, as described in the float rod section (page 32), and fit the reel fittings while doing so. The rings Les uses for his own rods are again the High Bells variety finished in hard chrome, and in size 1. For the butt ring he prefers a size 8 High Bells ring either lined with Aqualite or Sintox. The tip ring will be of the stand off Hepton variety threaded at the end of the tube to take the swing tip or quiver tips. The ring is again lined with Aqualite or Sintox. The rings are now whipped on using the following spacings. Reading from the tip of the top section and the base of the spigot or the butt section (in inches): top section 6¼, 8, 9, 12, 13½; butt section 10.

Whippings are again placed at the base of the top section and the base of the spigot or the butt section, and all are sealed and varnished. The finish and appearance of the above mentioned blanks is quite suitable as it is, but if required they can be varnished to give a gloss finish. The choice is yours.

CARP ROD

For our next rod we will move up the scale slightly to what is commonly known as the Mk IV design carp rod. This is a 10 ft two-piece rod with a 1½ lb test curve. Since its design in cane by Richard Walker it has become the standard carp rod. Blanks for this type of rod are readily available from almost all tackle shops. The finished rod is designed to fish with lines in the range of 6–11 lb b.s. It is capable of handling large fish such as carp or pike and also makes a first-class rod for salmon spinning. The blanks recommended for this rod are the ones made by Fibatube.

The handle is again made from cork, using any of the methods previously described. If you intend using the rod as a bit of an all-rounder, e.g. pike, as a spinning rod, it would be wise to incorporate a screw winch type reel fitting into the handle. If this is your requirement, here is the procedure. First, find out the best position for the fitting by taping the reel to the blank to help you decide. When the position is decided, mark the blank and fit corks on the lower end of the blank up to the marked position. Now the reel fitting is slid over the blank until it comes down to the fitted corks. The fitting will probably require packing, as the bore of it will be greater than the blank. The best way to do this is to take thin strips of wood the same length as the fitting and glue these side by side lengthwise around the blank. The size of these strips of wood in general will be approximately $6 \times \frac{3}{16} \times \frac{1}{16}$ in. Use Araldite to glue these in position and leave to set; when set, slide on the reel fitting. If it will not go over the glued strips sand these off with glasspaper until a good tight fit is ensured. Now remove the fitting again and refit with Araldite glue.

Fit further corks above the reel fitting for approximately 5–6 in. above the reel fitting. The total length of the handle on this rod needs to be 26–28 in., occasionally 30 in., depending on your own physique. The handle can now be shaped and finished as described on pages 17–24.

The rings used on this type of rod are what is known as 'Low Cradle Bridge'. Again, the hard chrome variety are preferred, using a size 14 or 16 Aqualite-lined Cradle Bridge ring for the butt, and a low pattern, lined end ring. The spacings, again reading from the top are (in inches): top section 7, 9, $10\frac{1}{2}$, 13; butt section $12\frac{1}{2}$. Whippings are placed at the base of the top section and the base of the spigot or the butt section. All ring whippings are sealed and varnished and the rod finished in gloss or matt to suit.

PIKE ROD

It would be logical now to move on to the next rod in our selection, this being the 10 ft two-piece rod suitable for pike fishing. This would be a rod capable of casting live baits and deadbaits good distances. The blanks used for this type of rod are quite commonly known as stepped up carp blanks. In these blanks the test curve can be 2 lb, 2½ lb, 2¾ lb or 3 lb. You will have to decide on your own particular requirements and select the blank accordingly. Obviously, the higher the test curve the more powerful the blank. To give the beginner a guide the most commonly used blank is the 2½–2¾ lb test curve, and this is certainly very suitable for most pike fishing. All the fittings for this rod will be exactly as described above in building a carp rod. The ring spacing will also be the same.

SPINNING ROD

No selection of rods would be complete without the inclusion of a spinning rod. Here we will go for a general purpose rod rather than a special purpose item. The length preferred seems to be 8½ ft, a size which gives scope for a fair range of spinning situations and bait sizes. Blanks for this type of rod are easily obtained and again the Fibatube range is good. The blanks are two-piece and hollow glass.

Fly rods

8 ft	4¼	5½	6¾	8	9½	10¾	12¾	14¾
8½ ft	5	6¾	8½	10½	12	12¼	12½	13
9 ft	4½	5¾	7¼	8¾	10¼	11½	11¾	12½	12½
9½ ft	4¾	6¼	7¾	9½	11¼	12	12¾	13¼	13¾

Spinning rods

8 ft	4¾	6¼	8	9	12¼	16¾
9 ft	5¼	7½	9½	12	14¼	16¾
10 ft	5¾	8¾	10¾	12¼	13¼	13¾	14¾

Ring spaces (in inches) for varying lengths of rod, in each case reading from the tip.

The rings and fittings will be exactly the same as used on the carp rod described previously. The reel fitting used should be of the screw type. Again, the fitting of the handle and reel fitting is exactly as described earlier. One small addition to the handle preferred on spinning rods is the butt cap, which is in the form of a tapered metal cone fitted to the base of the handle. To do this the corks are tapered off to match the taper of the butt cap, the butt cap then being glued into position over them. When set, a rod button can be screwed into the threaded base of the butt cap. The ring spacings are, reading from the top and from the base of the spigot on the butt section (in inches): top $6\frac{1}{2}$, 7, 9, 10, 11; butt section 8. All whippings to rings and strengthening whippings at the base of the top section and the base of the spigot on butt section are sealed and varnished to finish off.

FLY RODS

With the growth of stillwater trout fishing over recent years the making of a fly rod soon becomes a reality for many anglers. The fly rod is one of the *easiest* rods to make and could provide an ideal starting point for the angler wishing to make a rod. The tackle trade has a wealth of fly rod blanks available. Again, lengths and line size variations are numerous, but for a good general purpose rod suitable for most stillwater fishing we would choose a length of 9 ft or 9 ft 3 in., taking a size 7 or 8 line. Fibatube market a blank of 9 ft 3 in., taking both 7 and 8 lines, which makes an ideal rod. Other good blanks are also available from Cono-flex, Marco and North Western.

Having obtained a suitable blank we find that the short cork handle required can be purchased ready turned and sanded to shape. They are also available bored to varying sizes, enabling a ready-made handle to be purchased to fit most chosen blanks. Reel fittings are available in varying styles either in metal or lightweight plastic. Rings for fly rods are available also in varying patterns. The most commonly used are the 'snake' variety followed by the Low Cradle Bridge rings and the Fuji single leg variety. The Fuji type assist casting greatly as their frictionless centres allows line to flow through them easily. They are however, prone to easy damage. Of the other types mentioned we prefer the single loop 'snake' rings, again in hard chrome finish. Tip rings used are of the glue-on type and butt rings are hard chrome Cradle Bridge pattern.

The assembly of the rod begins with the fitting of the reel seating to the base of the butt section. Reel fittings are available in $\frac{5}{8}$ in. or $\frac{3}{4}$ in. diameter and one can usually be found to fit most blanks. Rather than pack the blank up too much to accommodate a $\frac{3}{4}$ in. reel fitting, we prefer to cut back the base of the blank to the length of the small reel fittings. Then, using a piece of thinner glass tube, fit a spigot into the base of the cut end of the rod blank. This is glued in position with Araldite and the fitting in turn is Araldited to the spigot.

The blank above the fitting is now roughed up with a file or glasspaper for the length the handle will cover. A ready-made cork handle is now slid down the blank and glued in position tight up to reel fitting. If the bore of the handle has to be opened up slightly this can be done with glasspaper wrapped round a smaller diameter piece of spare glass or dowel rod. Allow everything to set before continuing further.

The next operation is the fitting of the rings. One important point here is to ensure that the butt ring, and subsequently the following ring on the butt section, is in alignment with the reel position on the reel fitting. The best way to ensure this is to put a reel in the fitting. The ring positions (in inches) are for the 9 ft 3 in. rod we are making: top section 6, 6, $6\frac{1}{2}$, 8, $8\frac{1}{2}$, $11\frac{1}{2}$; butt section $5\frac{1}{8}$, 18.

If purchasing a blank of different length your tackle dealer will be able to give these positions or you can refer to the table on page 38. For ring spacing given in all cases read from the tip downward and from the spigot of the butt section towards the handle. Whippings, as in all previous rods, are placed at the base of the spigot on the butt section and at the base of the top section. All whippings are sealed and varnished to finish.

If you wish to follow modern trends and embark on the assembly of a carbon fibre fly rod, then all that has been written about a glass rod will apply to carbon fibre. The tackle trade is also aware of this trend and has made available cork handles and reel fittings with smaller diameter bores to meet the requirements of the carbon fibre blanks. Of the carbon fibre blanks available for the home rod builder the most popular are Lamiglass, but other good blanks are also available. In selecting the action of a carbon fibre blank remember they will always appear much stiffer than when loaded with line in actual fishing situations. All blanks will be marked with recommended line sizes.

For the last two rods in the range selected we turn to the sea. We will begin by assembling a 12 ft surf casting rod and complete this section with the construction of a 7 ft boat rod.

TWELVE-FOOT SURF CASTING ROD

Choosing a blank for your beachcaster will be greatly influenced by your casting ability. If you have never done any beach casting, or very little, then it would be unwise at this stage to buy a blank with a very fast-tapered tip. The fast-tapered blanks are very precise in their action and give no leeway in casting techniques. If this will be your first beachcasting rod we suggest you go for a more moderately tapered blank or even a reverse taper which will give a slow, leisurely cast. Blanks in these types can be found in the Fibatube, Cono-flex and North Western ranges. The casting weight range 4–6 oz is general.

Having selected our blank the next important point to establish is the position of the reel and the upper hand grips. Each person, being of different build, will obviously have a different 'comfortable' position. Most anglers cast best when the hands are placed roughly shoulder width apart. This position should give an upper hand position approx. 28–32 in. from the butt end. Mark this position on the rod with a pencil. This upper hand position is a very important factor in relation to the total length of the rod. If you find that you cannot apply full power to the rod in casting with hands at this position then either the rod is too long for you or the weight you are casting is too great. It is more often a small factor like handle length that prevents anglers achieving greater distance. Being in the position of building your own rod you have the golden opportunity to get it right, so there is time for experiment. Try different hand positions and weights before you fix anything permanently. To carry out these trials, simply tape on rod rings with sellotape in the positions given later. The reel can also be taped in position.

When you are happy with all the above, the permanent work can begin. The first task should be the whipping of the rings. The rings to be used will be of the braced High Bridge variety, again in hard chrome finish and the lightweight pattern. For the whipping use nylon in the heavy grade (size 15). Ring positions are as follows: reading from the tip (in inches) $5\frac{1}{2}$, $9\frac{1}{2}$, 11, 12, $13\frac{1}{4}$, $13\frac{1}{2}$; butt 10. For the butt ring it is not essential to use a different pattern unless one is using a fixed spool reel. The ring used then should be of larger diameter, say about 2–$2\frac{1}{2}$ in., to act as a coil breaker. Whippings are again placed at the base of the top section and at the top of the butt section, close to where the spigot emerges. These whippings should be at least $1\frac{1}{2}$ in. in length. The tip ring should be lightweight and the glue-on type is preferable. For the reel fitting we recommend the strap Fuji pattern. This is placed on the blank and held in position with whippings, one at each end, as for a rod rings, and two more across the fittings in the depressions provided for the same.

The hand grips are the next items and these are of rubber, as sold for motor-cycle handle grips. Most tackle shops sell these in different sizes. You will require two of one size for the two upper hand grips, one in front of the reel fitting and one immediately behind. The latter is the important one, the position of which you will have calculated through trial and error. A larger grip is slipped over the base of the blank to give the lower hand grip. As an extra, the length of blank between the hand grips can be covered in black shrink tubing. This is placed in position before the hand grips. Simply slip it over the blank and then hold it in front of an electric fire, not too close. It will then shrink tight on to the blank. The hand grips are then slipped into position, covering the ends of the shrink tubing. Finally, all whippings are sealed and given at least three coats of good varnish to prevent abrasion by sand and rocks. When carrying out the whipping of the rings be sure to pull the nylon very tight to ensure a secure grip on the rings.

SEVEN-FOOT BOAT ROD

A boat rod is the last of our selection of rods. Again the construction does not require a great deal of skill, for all parts can be purchased in a ready-to-fit state. Most boat rod blanks are sold in I.G.F.A. class ratings, i.e. 12, 20, 30, 50 and 80 lb class. What class you require will be determined by the locality you fish and the quarry you seek to catch. If required for cod on the east coast then a 20 lb class would cope with most fishing situations. On the other hand, if required for wreck fishing off the south-west coasts then something of 50–80 lb class should be considered.

For the object of this exercise we will assemble a 20 lb class rod and we begin by making up the handle. This can be in the form of a ready-made beechwood handle or a piece of $\frac{7}{8}$ in. diameter glass or alloy tube. We have a personal preference for glass, but to whichever handle you choose we have to fit the reel fitting. The one to use is the Modlock fitting marketed by Modern Arms Co. (Marco) and available from good tackle shops. You require this with a $\frac{7}{8}$ in. diameter size. This fitting has the screw-locking counter ferrule as part of it, allowing the handle to be removed from the rod. The reel fitting is glued to the top of the handle (the wooden handle having been turned down ready to accept it). When glueing with Araldite, remove the counter ferrule and push the fitting on the handle almost to the cross pin inside the fitting. *This cross pin must be kept clean of all glue.* The counter ferrule has two cut-away portions at its base which locates the cross pin to prevent twisting. To the bottom of the handle is fitted a butt cap and a screw-in rubber button. If making up a blank of 30 lb class and above, it would be advisable to fit a cross slot gimbal for use with a butt pad.

With the lower handle now complete we turn our attention to the blank. The base of this is glued with Araldite into the counter ferrule section of the reel fitting. Be careful to ensure it remains central while glueing as it is smaller in diameter than the inside of the ferrule. One method we use successfully is to put ample glue in the ferrule, push the blank into it and then insert match-sticks down between the two. About six matchsticks, evenly spaced, are sufficient. Then let it stand and allow to set. With the ferrule securely fitted our next task is to make a small hand grip above it, generally about 6 in. in length. This is done with handle corks. These are slid down the blank and glued side by side, starting close up to the ferrule. Put on enough corks to make up the required length. When set, sand the corks to the desired shape. This generally tapers slightly towards the top.

The main job remaining now is to whip on the rings. The pattern of ring used for this rod is the Cradle Bridge, in Diamite finish. This is one of the hardest rings available. The ring positions are, reading from the top (in inches), 4, 4½, 6, 7, 8, 10. The top ring, again in Diamite, is of the glue-on variety. All intermediate rings should be whipped with heavy duty nylon (size 15) and sealed and varnished. The important point to remember when positioning rings is to ensure they are in alignment with the reel position on the reel fitting. One final task is to varnish the handle if the beechwood type was used.

By using the Modlock fitting it is possible to make up a series of different class tops, i.e. 12, 30, 50 lb and all be interchangeable on the existing handle. This is made possible by the fact that Modern Arms Co. market the counter ferrule, through tackle dealers, as a separate item.

*   *   *   *

With the selection of rods detailed in the previous pages and used in conjunction with the specialised chapters earlier we hope we have guided you well enough to want to take on the task of assembling at least one rod and so add another pleasure to your angling activities.

REPAIRING RODS

It is generally recognised that one of the first D.I.Y. tasks undertaken by the angler is the repair of a broken rod. What Les Beecroft proposes to do in this section is to set out some methods for the repair of rods of various construction and materials.

CRUSHED FIBRE GLASS

This is a common occurrence and is usually caused by rods being pushed too tightly into roll-up holdalls and the straps being excessively strained. It arises, too, from holdalls being stacked on top of one another on angling buses. In both cases the end result is the rings of one rod pressing against another and crushing the glass over a small section. Such mishaps would not occur if rods were carried in tubes inside the holdall, and lengths of $2\frac{1}{2}$ in. diameter plastic drainpipe are ideal for such a purpose. However, with the damage done, how do we repair it?

Let us assume for this exercise that the problem is 6 in. above the handle on the butt section and that the rod is crushed on one side for a length of 3 in. First remove the butt cap: this will either be of the plastic type or alloy, and in each case it will have been glued to the corks of the handle. Cut round the corks close to the top edge of the butt cap right down to the glass blank and by careful levering with the knife the corks under the butt cap will break away from the glass blank, allowing the butt cap to be removed. Either clean out the butt cap for replacement later or discard it and buy a new one. With the butt cap removed you now have access to the inside of the blank.

The next job is to measure the diameter of the rod $1\frac{1}{2}$ in. below the crushed section. From this measurement subtract $\frac{1}{16}$ in. and this will allow for the wall thickness of the blank. This will, for our purpose, give us an inside diameter accurate enough to work from. From your local model makers' shop obtain a piece of hard balsa dowel of suitable diameter to the inside measurement. You will be lucky if you find a piece to your exact requirements, so buy a nearest size larger. Cut a 6 in. length from this dowel.

Next, measure the rod diameter again, this time $1\frac{1}{2}$ in. above the damaged section and subtract $\frac{1}{16}$ in. from the first measurement obtained. We now realise we have to form a 6 in. long slightly tapered plug from our 6 in. length of balsa wood. This will present no problems to the reader with access to a lathe or an electric drill. For those less fortunate we suggest the best way is to sand the *ends* of the balsa down, turning it all the time down to the required measurements. When this is done, remove the excess in the centre, maintaining the required taper. Always wrap your glasspaper around a wide piece of plywood, or something similar, as this will help to give the even taper. To preserve its cylindrical shape, turn the dowell all the time you are working. With the dowel plug prepared, offer it up inside the blank from the bottom; it will need a push with some sort of thin rod. It should come to rest under the damaged section and extend beyond each end of it for approximately $1\frac{1}{2}$ in. If the plug gets

too tight before reaching this point, push it out again by inserting your push rod from the spigot end. You will now have to
sand off some more from the dowel plug. Be careful not to take
off too much. It takes very little to move the plug an inch up the
blank.

Now we trust we have our balsa plug suitably prepared.
Using Araldite, work this glue into the cracks and any broken
fibres at the crushed section. Take your plug and coat its entire
length with Araldite *but not all round it.* Coat just half of the
circumference. Now we come to inserting it up the inside of the
blank and the reason for not coating the plug all round. Lay the
plug inside the blank with it resting on the uncoated side. It
can now be pushed carefully into position without leaving all
your glue on the inside of the blank, everywhere but where it is
needed. When the plug is in the required position (if you hold the
rod up to a strong light you will be able to see the shadow made
by the plug) you only need to twist it 360° to ensure you get a
coating of glue all round the plug.

To achieve this we use a length of dowel rod as a push rod, into
the end of which we have drilled a hole and inserted a screw
with the head cut off. The screw is fixed in the dowel with Araldite, with its thread projecting $\frac{3}{4}$ in. Before inserting the half-
coated plug into the blank we first screw it on the end of the
dowel rod. Thus we are able to distribute the glue by turning
the dowel clockwise when the plug is in its correct position. A
few anti-clockwise turns release the push rod, leaving the plug
in place.

With the plug in position, take some fine strong thread and
bind the section of rod tightly over the length of the plug. These
turns of thread can be openly spaced as long as they are tight;
they are only temporary. This binding should cause any surplus glue to be forced up through the cracks in the damaged
area. Wipe the excess away and leave all to set. If using normal
Araldite about 24 hours is sufficient. With all set, remove your
temporary bindings and clean off the required section with the
use of *fine* glasspaper. This done, and using rod whipping silk of
the colour to match the other rod whippings, whip the whole
repaired section in close turns as if whipping a rod eye. Finish
off with dope and varnish to match the rod.

The reason for using balsa dowel for this type of repair is that it gives enough support to the crushed area without building in a rigid section to the rod, as would be the case with a piece of spare fibre glass. During my years as a tackle dealer I have repaired many rods with this method and all have proved totally satis-factory. The method can be used at any point on a hollow glass rod for the crushed type of damage, but not if a total break has occurred.

THE BROKEN GLASS JOINT

This quite common form of damage can be repaired if it is con-fined to a short section of the rod. It will be beyond repair if con-siderable crushing has also been done, as would happen if the rod had been trodden on! The damage we are dealing with in this section is a total break with splitting of the broken ends occur-ring for a length of no more than 2 in. from the break. For this exercise we will assume the break is in the middle section of a 13 ft match rod.

Our first task is to mark on each broken piece the extremity of the splitting. This done, we must now cut the blank at this point. Cutting must be done with a fine-toothed saw and must be absolutely square. Our next task is to obtain a spare piece of glass fibre of the same taper as the damaged section. We require a length of glass of approximately 6 in. A suitable piece of glass can be obtained if you take the prepared broken pieces to your tackle dealer, for most dealers carrying out rod repairs will have a supply of glass pieces obtained from broken rods. With our piece of glass to hand, rough it up with coarse glasspaper before offering it up inside from the lower end of the blank. It should fit snugly at the broken end and protrude for 3 in. If this is not the case, sand with glasspaper until it will so fit.

Using Araldite glue and the same glueing technique as des-cribed in the previous repair, glue the piece of glass into the lower broken section. You will now have a section with a spigot extending from the top. Bind the section temporarily over the glued section and wipe off any glue squeezed from the end. Take the prepared top section and push this down on the spigot (no glue) and check the alignment of the rod section. Do not worry if the prepared top section does not go right down on the spigot at this stage: it is the alignment that is of paramount

21 and 22 Repair of damaged glass blanks, illustrating the text.

importance. If this is satisfactory, place everything to one side and allow to set. Then, with glue set and spigot firmly glued in the lower section, make any final adjustment needed to the other section to ensure it fits snugly on the spigot and that the two prepared ends of the broken section butt up tight.

Having confirmed this, coat the spigot with Araldite and push on the top section, re-checking the alignment. Bind with thread temporarily, wipe off any surplus glue, and place to one side to set. When all is set, remove the temporary bindings and clean up the repaired section. Close-whip with silk to match the other rod bindings and finish off with dope and varnish. Although your rod section will be approximately 4 in. shorter you will have certainly saved the cost of a new section of rod.

BROKEN SPIGOT

Having read the above the reader will soon recognise the fact that to complete this repair he has simply to follow the same instructions. They are followed to the point where the 6 in. piece of glass is glued into the base and left to set. When all is set, offer the top section of the rod to the spigot. This should become tight on the spigot with the ends of the rod sections remaining approx. $\frac{1}{4}$–$\frac{1}{8}$ in. apart. Should it not fit to the spigot this far, remove it and sand the spigot gently all round with glasspaper until this situation is reached. If the top section is still loose on the spigot when the ends have butted up, then remove it and with a fine-toothed saw cut approximately $\frac{1}{8}$ in. from the base of the top section, making sure that the cut is square. This procedure may be repeated, removing small sections from the base of the top section, until the desired fit is achieved. With rod-whipping silk, replace the whippings at the base of the top section. These whippings should have a span of approximately 1 in. Finally, remove the temporary bindings from the lower section of the rod and replace them with rod-whipping silk for approximately 1 in., starting as close as possible to the point where the spigot emerges.

What has been written about repairs to hollow glass rods will also apply to breaks of the same nature in carbon fibre rods. With solid glass rods there is no really satisfactory way of making a repair. In the short term, the broken sections can be sleeved on the outside and bound tightly, but the repair is far from permanent and scarcely justifies the effort.

BUILT CANE REPAIRS

Cane usually breaks in one of two ways. First with what we call a 'green-stick' break. This is where the cane breaks part the way through and then splits along its length. We will deal with this first because it is the easier of the two.

Open up the break, clean, and using a waterproof woodworking glue, coat all inside surfaces including both sides of any separated fibres of cane. By bending the rod joint it will be easier to get the glue to the extremities of the longitudinal splits. When all the surfaces are coated with glue, bind the damaged section with open spiral windings in both directions. Check that the section is straight and place it aside to allow the glue to set. During the setting period check frequently to see the section remains straight. With the glue set, remove the temporary binding and clean off the surplus glue and the cane generally. The next task is to whip the repaired section in close turns with silk, matching the other rod whippings. To achieve a near invisible mend this close whipping can be carried out with clear monofilament; 4 lb b.s. will be found to be the best size.

The other break in cane that is much more difficult to repair is the clean break. This also applies to that older rod building material, greenheart. The rod can only be repaired successfully if it is spliced. This can be done if you are prepared to be unhurried and to take great care. The tools you will need are a very sharp hand plane (cane is a very hard wood) and some glasspaper wrapped around a flat block of wood. Also required is a fine-toothed saw.

We begin by sawing off the splintered ends of the sections to be spliced. These ends must be overlapped for a considerable length. If it is a top section about 1½ in. would be sufficient, but for a butt section twice this length would be more suitable. With the ends overlapped, mark the sections of cane where the ends terminate. We now come to the careful part of the job, for each section has to be tapered off equally back to the marks we have placed, leaving us with the ends of the two sections looking like two identical wedges placed back to back. The difficulty will be found in keeping the two tapered surfaces absolutely flat and even. If one is tapered more steeply than the other you will end up with a bent rod on completion. On the other hand, if the tapered surface is not parallel with the underside flat section of cane you will end up with a twisted rod joint. The importance of these angles cannot be over-stressed and great care must be taken.

To check before actual glueing, we suggest that you tape the splice together with sellotape and check the alignment. When you are satisfied that all is in order, coat both flat tapered surfaces with a thin coat of waterproof working glue and bind them together with temporary bindings. Check again for alignment before putting the work aside for the glue to set – but continue to check the alignment from time to time. Leave the job for at least 24 hours to make sure the glue has really set, then remove the temporary windings and clean off any surplus glue. Clean up the cane generally and prepare for whipping. Starting at least ½ in. before the join, whip the whole spliced area, finishing ½ in. beyond the repair. Use rod-whipping silk to match or clear monofilament, as you wish. Finally, varnish to finish.

This is a very good method of repairing a cane rod and many repaired several years ago are still giving good service. But the success of the repair lies in the good fitting of the overlapped joint: if this is badly prepared then the repair is destined to failure.

Finally, a few words on the subject of handles. It often happens that the corks get damaged or worn out, though only a small section in the middle of the handle may be affected. It is not necessary to remove all the handle corks to carry out this repair. Use a very sharp knife to cut around the join of the last damaged cork at each end of the damaged section. Cut down until the glass or cane is felt beneath the blade. When you have done this, cut off the damaged corks, working from the centre towards the cuts you have made around the handle. The end result should be a cleaned-out section of handle with the good section of corks being cleanly cut at each end. Select the same number of corks as you have removed and again using the sharp knife cut through one side of them. Now, using a waterproof adhesive, coat the uncovered section of handle and both sides of the first cork. Open out the split in the cork and place a thin coat of glue on both surfaces. By holding the split in the cork open with both hands you will be able to spring it over the uncovered handle sections and push it into place tight up against the good section of cork handle. If a particular ring breaks it was probably a bad one anyway, so choose another. Repeat the operation until the damaged section is completely replaced. Bind corks together and leave for the glue to set. Finally, remove the temporary bindings and sand the new corks down to the same level of the existing handle.

Rod and reel maintenance

SECOND-HAND RODS AND REELS

The second-hand market in fishing tackle is always lively and few weeks go by without a long list of 'bargains' being offered for sale or exchange in the classified advertisements of the angling press. Undoubtedly a great deal of excellent tackle is offered, and this is one way of stocking up without a considerable amount of expense. But there is also a fair amount of 'odd' pieces offered for sale, and a few well-chosen words and practical hints may help to prevent an angler purchasing that expensive pig-in-a-poke which would eventually join the 'has beens' in the tackle armoury.

From the outset we would make it clear that the second-hand market is not the best starting point for the lone angler new to the sport. Grand though the advertisements extolling the 'complete beginners' outfit' may sound, and sound though the reasons given for its sale may be, the novice will, in many instances, be putting his neck into a noose. Far better is the tackle shop and its owner, who will offer a range of rods and reels that can be tried and tested so that a balanced rod and reel can be selected. Someone else's complete outfit may look great at the time, but prove completely unbalanced and useless to its new owner on the bankside.

An ideal way for the novice to start is by borrowing and using two or three types of rod from friends, so that he can select the one that suits him best. From that point the beginner will know exactly what he wants, and can look for and be able to price it on the second-hand market with an accurate eye. Don't get us wrong – we are not suggesting that the second-hand market is full of sharks waiting to 'clean up' on the unsuspecting by foisting off rubbish. But it is all too easy to set out wanting one thing, and through enthusiasm and lack of knowledge, finishing up with that which is totally unsuitable.

With a clear knowledge of one's requirements the advertisements can be studied and a series of eliminations practised. Part-exchange deals in advertisements where the vendor is looking for snow-shoes and a pair of breeding ferrets are best left alone. Advertisements where the vendor is a long way from the purchaser can also be ruled out. Despite some of the deposit systems offered by a few magazines to safeguard money transactions, the physical effort and unnecessary expense of sending tackle backwards and forwards is a fag that can often result in damage to items – especially where rods are sent by road or rail, a necessary method where the Post Office enforces a parcel size limit of about three feet or so in length.

Naturally one wants to inspect something before a possible purchase, and if it is a rod then the only time to do that is during the day, and somewhere with sufficient space that will enable the item to be assembled; more especially this applies if a fly rod is being examined and its action assessed.

More fishing tackle has been purchased on the spur of the moment without a first thought – let alone a second – than bears thinking about. To help with those second thoughts we have prepared a check list for various items, together with faults and how to search for them.

RODS

Some of the faults that can appear in wooden rods have already been listed under the heading of materials. But how to find them is another story. Start by laying the joints out, side by side, and comparing the length of each of them. If a butt or middle joint appears shorter than the rest, or the top joint appears unusually short, then it is an odds-on chance that there has been a break at some time, and the damaged parts repaired by levelling off and re-ferruling or by fitting a new spigot. When in doubt – ask for a tape measure and use it. If an 11 ft rod measures only 10 ft 10 in. then it is on the cards that a bit is missing – and that could materially affect the rod's action, especially if it is a casting rod.

Next, examine the butt cap and winch fittings, checking for

tightness and possible wear, especially with screw winch fittings; a reel that is sloppy in its fitment to the rod can be guaranteed to part company when least expected or wanted. Worn and cracked corks may not be the ends of the earth where faults are concerned, but they will need replacement or repair, along with badly fitting butt accoutrements, and it would be reasonable to expect a cash adjustment to allow for these.

Check rod rings for wear visually, and when some scoring appears, or where any of the various types of agate ring have been used, make a physical check by running a pin point around the bearing surface. The slightest crack (capable of ruining a line in seconds) can be felt.

Ferrules in most instances appear round to the eye, usually because we expect them to be so. But often, through an accumulation of dirt, the male will not couple fully with its female counterpart. After a period of time this slack fitting will produce strain and the ferrule will pull into an oval shape, ultimately acquiring 'slop' and play. The easiest way to check this fault (one especially prevalent in older rods) is to run a lead pencil point around the female ferrule edge, then push a thick piece of paper flush against the blackened edge. If the ferrule has become oval it will be seen immediately.

Sometimes the ferrule lip can be tapped back into shape, or the ferrule replaced with one of a similar type. Either way, it could end up as an expense, or worse, a gamble. Loose ferrules will require re-setting – not an exceptionally hard job (see the instructions on page 12) providing that the wood underneath is sound.

Having examined the ferrules, offer the joints up and make sure that they sheet home. Then place a hand about 8 in. above and the other 8 in. below the connected ferrules at each joint in turn, grasp the wood firmly, and slop the rod up and down. Wear in the fittings not normally discernible when the rod is used in the conventional way can be felt immediately.

Now examine the timber of the rod. Split cane can, with age, work loose – the glue breaks down, more especially when the rod is steel-centred. Look along each joint and view with suspicion any wide gaps. Whole cane that is 'breaking up' usually begins with small cracks between the nodes, which spring apart if the rod is heavily flexed. Lancewood and greenheart usually give no signs of imminent fracture – but look for a prior break that has been spliced, glued and whipped. No complete break is ever 100 per cent in strength after repair.

The final check is for trueness and temper. With all the joints assembled (outside in the open if possible) sight along the rod from butt to tip, the tip being held against a light background – the sky is ideal. Note how straight the rod is; if there is a slight bend, or set as it is called, downwards, in the direction in which a fish would be played, then all is well. If the set is pronounced in this direction it can be cured by removing the rod rings, turning the winch fittings over if they are of the fixed variety, and then re-whipping the rod rings on the reverse side of the rod. In time wear will return the set, and straighten things again.

There is a tendency for split cane to become 'soft' with age – in other words the temper leaves each segment that makes up the complete joint, and it will remain bent into whichever direction it is strained. There is no cure other than replacement of the joint itself with a new one. Yes, you are quite right, we have mentioned some of these faults earlier, but with the price of second-hand cane rods running into the £50–£60 bracket we make no apologies for a second reminder of faults that may well present a bad purchase.

By now you will have a firm idea of the flaws that the rod contains, and it will be possible to categorise them precisely. Cane opening with age, and rods that are soft should be left strictly alone. They can be repaired, but the cost of the work together with the purchase price may not prove an economical investment.

Re-ringing, replacement of odd rings or ferrules (providing that a replacement is available; the era of the spigot seeming to have ousted most of them) are all jobs that are within the scope of the average angler and a suitable bartering point over price with the vendor.

Most people give glass fibre a perfunctory glance when they are offered such a rod. The idea that the material is indestructible and that rods so made will withstand anything still persists. Good though glass fibre is, it can still, with time, assume a set, although this of course can be cured by re-ringing. Occasionally some of the thin-walled blanks can fracture, usually in the form of hair-line cracks. But most trouble where glass fibre is concerned occurs around the spigot. Over-forcing the female joint on the male spigot can either cause small cracks at the edge of the female joint, or wear down the spigot itself to such an extent that both male and female parts butt against each other, and the joint becomes loose. Cutting back the female ferrule is the cure, a small job that does not detract from the value of the rod. Cracks around the spigot, however, are a different matter and our opinion is that such rods are best left alone.

One final thought on the action of rods is worth mentioning. If a fly rod is being examined and very sensibly tried, it is worth remembering that the action of such a rod becomes softer and easier with age. This means that the weight of line for which it was originally manufactured becomes too heavy and the whole rod feels out of balance. A size lighter line will often improve the action of the rod beyond all belief; but whether this is an acceptable argument for a reduction in price is debatable.

REELS

There are two types of reel available on the second-hand market – those that are in current production, and those older models that are no longer made, but which still soldier on. The division between the two is an important one and must largely affect the value of the item.

Some general rules on reel examination apply equally to both old and new. Whilst their overall appearance may look good, the wearing point in all reels will obviously lie along the centre spindle (or pin) in the case of fly reels or multipliers and around the reciprocating spindle of fixed spool models. Hold the back plate of the reel firmly in one hand and check for side play by rocking the spool from side to side with the other hand, listening for clatter that denotes wear. If it is present then open the reel and check the amount of grease that is packed around the spindle. If there is none then apply a little, and re-check for wear again. If there is still an apparent rattle, then think twice before making an offer. Should the model still be in production then often a replacement spindle can be supplied or fitted – but older models leave the owner out on a limb; only one thing being certain – that the wear will get worse with age and use.

Fly reels with securing screws that have obviously never

been turned since the model left the factory often hide a worn check mechanism. At the other end of the scale, a fixed spool reel with a well worn drag adjusting screw mounted into the spool denotes that there is probably too large a gap between the spool and its metal housing through which line slips and twists around its innards. Another part in which to search for wear in a fixed spool reel is at the crook of the pick-up arm. Nylon turning against a solid piece of metal soon grooves it – and constant rubbing against the rib of the groove will, in turn, wear the line. Even the roller bearing on later models can jam with accumulated grit and lack of maintenance, so look for these signs of grooving yet again. There is little expense and inconvenience in replacing these small parts providing that they are still in production. If they are not – then leave the reel well alone.

Sea reels suffer more abuse than any other type of fishing reel. Most users assume that all parts on the reel will be corrosion-proof and accordingly treat the model to a minimum of attention. Worse still, they open the reel and cover everything inside with a liberal coating of thick grease to 'protect' it.

All that happens where this treatment is applied is that sand and grit combine with the grease to produce a super abrasive which wears the working parts in double-quick time. Moral: look carefully and, if necessary, strip and examine before purchasing. You are paying the price – if the vendor is unwilling to let you open things up, then something is surely wrong.

Cracked plastic bodywork and dented rims are usually obvious, and bent handles apparent to the touch. But above all, do remember our earlier rule – if it is old and out of production, then its life (as far as spares are concerned) can be short. New models may cost a little more, but will generally prove cheaper in the long run – especially when they receive regular maintenance.

OTHER ITEMS

Which leaves the miscellaneous, but no less expensive items of tackle that may be picked up second-hand. Umbrellas, tackle boxes, rod rests and clothing are very easily checked, and with the exception of umbrellas, fairly simple to repair.

But some items that can be offered are overlooked, usually because of their appearance. Spinning lures of all shapes and sizes are always worth a whirl; bodies can be cleaned; hooks, swivels, etc. replaced, and the whole thing tarted up. Plug baits are the same, although these rarely make an appearance in advertisements. But odd lots of fishing floats, especially the 'old timers' such as Thames floats, quills, etc. are often thrown in with a box or bag that is for sale, and these are definitely worth hanging on to. A little work with glasspaper and paint can make them look – and act – like new.

So, to sum up. The second-hand market is an excellent proposition as a money saver – providing you know exactly what you want to buy, and how to look for the faults that may appear in the items that are offered to you. Our golden rule, when confronted with a 'bargain' that we are uncertain about is the same as for overtaking in a car – 'when in doubt – hang back'.

REEL MAINTENANCE

The amount of regular maintenance, or maintenance of any sort, that is given to a reel is generally non-existent. Why this situation should be is a mystery. Most men change oil in their cars, sharpen the blades in their lawnmowers, and generally manage routine maintenance jobs around the house without reminder of any sort; but for some reason the fishing reel is expected to go on performing without attention.

There was a time when they were relatively inexpensive, and whilst not in the throw-away bracket at least were replaceable without the necessity of a second mortgage on the house. But today's prices – anything around and above £30 for a decent model, regardless of the style of fishing which it is intended for – demands a fair return for the initial outlay.

More important than the financial angle is the fact that a reel that ruptures whilst it is being used can ruin a day's fishing or lose a fish – all for the sake of fifteen minutes (at the most) of easy work. To excuse the job on the grounds that the reel 'isn't used very often' is only admissible if, after use, it is dried and stored in a case or bag that can be closed to exclude grit, dust, and general gunge that accumulates in fishing bags and boxes. Although no hard and fast rules can be laid down, a reel needs stripping and a thorough cleaning and greasing at least twice during a season – more if the reel is subjected to hard usage.

One cannot maintain any reel without proper tools, and we are not referring to the kitchen scissors and a nail-file under that heading. Screws can be ruined by an ill-fitting screwdriver, and nuts loosened by a pair of thin-nosed pliers soon acquire burred edges. Inevitably, it is always these points that lock and cause so much frustration.

Better class reels are provided with a multi-purpose tool designed to cope with various locking points on that particular

23 Tools and materials for reel stripping. Matched screwdrivers and proprietary reel manufacturers' tools are most used; the king-sized spanners are occasionally necessary. Oil and grease will both be required, and the egg-cup is used to hold small parts for cleaning with the lighter fuel.

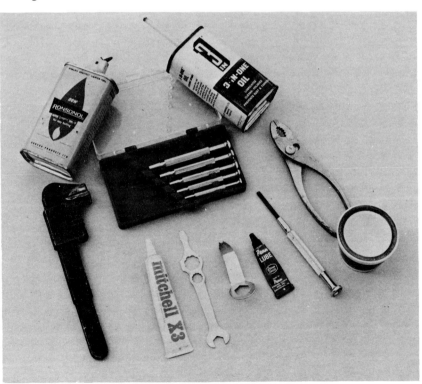

model. They are not designed to cope with another maker's reels and, if applied to them, can produce the sort of results we outlined earlier. For the angler with several reels to maintain the cheapest investment is a set of screwdrivers with steel-hardened tips and cased to prevent loss, together with a small adjustable spanner with fine jaws. To reinforce this array of tools there should also be a plentiful supply of clean, fluff-free rags.

Naturally one needs a supply of oil and grease with which to lubricate and pack bearings and surfaces. Again, many manufacturers provide their own lubricants, and these are better than some of the Vaseline-type greases and light machine oils that are often used. More important still is the fact that these are packed in tubes or containers that have an efficient nozzle, allowing the content to be placed exactly where it is required.

Given a good table with room to spread tools and parts as they are stripped, and a sensible light to illuminate the reel, the work of stripping can commence. Those anglers without a degree in engineering or an M.A. in Pelmanism will join with us in agreeing that the actual work of stripping is not in the least difficult; but putting the pieces together again is a different story altogether. Of course, if you have kept the maker's handbook supplied when the reel was new, then the job is comparatively easy; where this has been lost or the reel has been purchased as second-hand, then the problem of re-assembling will rear its ugly head. One answer to the problem is to start by photographing the reel before it is attacked – at least it gives you something to strive for! Then the operation can commence.

Working against a plain white background is the only way of ensuring that small screws, washers, springs and other little widgers are not lost as dismantling proceeds. The ideal system to follow is to remove each part, piece at a time, and place it in a line from the work centre, starting with part one some distance away and working backwards so that the last part stripped (and logically the first part needed for re-assembly) is immediately to hand. Once the parts are stretched out in a line it is a good time to take a second photograph which will provide a check-list for future reference of all the parts involved in the reel's various movements. The photo also helps if one has a piece over once the reel is (supposedly) put together, and is also a sure-fire way of re-ordering a spare part from the manufacturer.

Screws that are difficult to extract and may in fact appear jammed beyond possible release can sometimes be shifted by fitting a screwdriver into the screw head (making sure that the right thickness and width of blade is used – otherwise the slot will burr and finally rupture) and giving the handle a few sharp taps. Then turn the blade both clockwise and anti-clockwise in an attempt to gain some movement; not only will this often effect a cure, it will also allow the dreaded left-hand thread to identify itself to the operator. If this fails then one of the freeing oils will be the final resort, most of which are supplied in a spray aerosol can.

Not all of these liquids enjoy a happy relationship with fishing lines, so either the drum of the reel must be removed, or the line covered to protect it. Even worse, some metals used in reel construction become badly discoloured by these freeing agents. The answer to this problem is to release a little of the liquid into a saucer (away from the reel) and then to dab a small drop of it on an inconspicuous part of the reel with the help of a screwdriver blade. If no discolouration takes place, further amounts can be dropped around the screw head with the screw-driver blade as a transferring medium. Stubborn nuts are dealt with in the same manner, but especial care must be taken not to distort the shoulders, which will cause future attempts at releasing to become nigh on impossible.

Cleaning away old oil and grease can be done by using a piece of rag, lightly moistened with lighter fuel, and worked into corners with the aid of a matchstick. Dried grease, mud, grit and sands of the ages wedged into the rim of the spool and on the back plate, or under various open mechanisms are best tackled with a toothbrush and lighter fuel – the latter being given time to soak into the accumulated muck before the brushwork commences. Small springs, screws and metal (*but not fibre or nylon*) washers should be dropped into an egg cup and covered with lighter fuel, then dried with a fluff-free piece of rag, or *cold* air from a hair-drier. Fibre and nylon washers need a heavy rub with a cloth – and nothing else.

Lubrication should be given during re-assembly, taking care to contain it only to those areas where wear will occur. Contrary to the belief of many anglers, large amounts of grease and oil will not allow an extension of the period between servicing.

They merely encourage the accumulation of abrasive dust, sand, etc. – which, as we said earlier, will help to wear many parts long before they need be.

Naturally it is impossible to provide guidance on the maintenance of every reel ever produced, so we offer the following general hints under the various categories that the angler uses.

FIXED SPOOL REELS

Start by removing the tension screw (where fitted) in the front of the reel, then work backwards through tension springs, washer, and the spool itself, laying each item out in line. The cover plate to the body itself is generally held in place by three or four screws, allowing the plate and handle to be removed in one piece, and exposing the gear mechanism within the body pressing.

When new, the gear mechanism was grease-packed, but this

24 Spool and drag mechanism, plus the gear cover of a fixed spool reel stripped ready for cleaning and re-packing with grease.

will tend to disperse away from the cogs and thicken with age and use. It can be removed with a matchstick and cloth, the gears cleaned *in situ*, and then re-packed with grease. Once the cover plate is replaced and secured remember to apply a little light oil to the handle itself, then the spool and various washers with securing screw can be returned in their correct order.

The bail arm itself seldom gives trouble, and one should not attempt to remove it unless there is a mechanical fault, or a part is badly worn. Check that the roller bearing around which the nylon line is led runs freely, and is not clogged with grit. Apply a little light oil, and the job is done.

Dirt and grit is the natural enemy of all fixed spool reels, and it cannot be emphasised strongly enough that these items should always be packed in a box or bag when not in use. There are cheap, but very efficient zip bags on the market made especially for the purpose. Finally, if running maintenance is necessary on the bankside remember to do it over a clear surface where dropped pieces cannot be lost. A coat spread out, or even one's cap, makes an emergency bench.

CENTREPIN REELS

The introduction of automatic, fixed spool, and multiplying reels tended to oust the centrepin from its prime position in the angling world. But in recent years there has been a resurgence in its use, particularly in the match fisherman's armoury, as there has been to some lesser degree for the sea angler's boat rod.

Naturally the centrepin is the game fisherman's principal weapon, although even in this field there has been the introduction of multiplying and automatic mechanisms. These latter innovations can be quite complicated, especially where clockwork or spring operated models are concerned. From the outset we would make it clear that completely stripping and re-assembling automatic centrepins is a task best left to the tackle dealer or manufacturer; such drastic treatment is seldom easy, and in many instances special tools are needed to withdraw or re-set some of the working parts. Of course, regular maintenance tends to ward off the evil day when such treatment must take place.

Maintaining a fly reel takes but minutes. The drum is released from the back plate and spindle via the catch, release lever, button or, in some cases, centre screw that may be fitted. If there is a screw securing the drum – then remember our earlier warning of the dreaded left-hand thread! Strangely, this is one of the most delicate parts of the reel that usually works every time it is used. Should it not, it can be guaranteed to receive the maximum of physical force from fingers, and ultimately hammers and screwdrivers, ensuring permanent damage. Most release mechanisms jam through a mixture of accumulated and dried grease and grit. If the reel does not come apart, try a little petrol or one of the special easing fluids, with re-application over several days if necessary. Once the fluid has seeped through, then the various parts will separate easily.

Once apart the check and/or drag mechanism on the backplate of the reel will be exposed, in most instances consisting of a simple spring that can be tensioned to push a triangular shaped metal plate on to a ridged bush, which is fixed to the rear of the

25 Grease, sand and general filfth inside an otherwise useful Nottingham sea-reel. The screw shown, which mounts into the centre spindle, is of the dreaded left-hand variety. The large adjustable spanner was necessary to shift the retaining wing-nut.

spool. Nothing here presents great difficulty – a clean with some petrol and a cloth, some oil on the moving parts, and then, after the spindle of the reel has been oiled, the parts can be re-assembled.

If the check plate is worn, a replacement can be obtained from the manufacturers or cut from a piece of hard metal and mounted – the work of seconds. Some of the better quality reels have a spare check plate mounted by means of a screw on the backplate. Wear on the bush set at the rear of the spool necessi-tates return to the manufacturer for a replacement unit to be fitted. If the reel is out of production, then cast around for some-thing similar in the junk line, and try to marry it in. Quite often a tackle dealer has a reel brought in for repair that is beyond redemption, and a note together with a sketch of the part you require can result in his 'buying-in' one of these 'smash-ups' for your spares.

Yet another area where severe wear can occur is against the bottom space and bracing bars, which support the outer frame-work. Constant stripping of line from the reel causes wear

26 This wooden centrepin was dropped, breaking a large section off the lip of the drum. The repair from a shaped piece of non-corrosive alloy, together with new bases to the handles, has restored it to full use.

marks to appear in the metal, especially when this is a soft alloy. Occasionally the grooves that are produced by this action can be cured in the early stages by a little careful filing with a very fine, round file – but eventually the body of the reel will itself need replacement. Prevention is definitely cheaper than cure where this occurs – it is, in our experience, only an occasional fault, caused by the angler pulling backwards as well as downwards when pulling line free. Time spent in curing the backward part of the pulling motion when casting will obviate such wear altogether.

Centrepin reels for coarse fishing and spinning (yes – some of them still exist, and wonderful examples of engineering they are) have come back into fashion again, although it must be admitted that the spinning reels are now more usually used in coarse fishing, especially in the field of carp and competition work. They are dealt with in the same way as the fly fisherman's reel where maintenance is concerned, with a little extra care being taken to prevent too much oil flooding into the working

27 Dust and grease around the check mechanism on a modern freshwater centrepin reel. If it cannot be cleared with petrol or similar suitable solvent, try the pressure airline at your local garage.

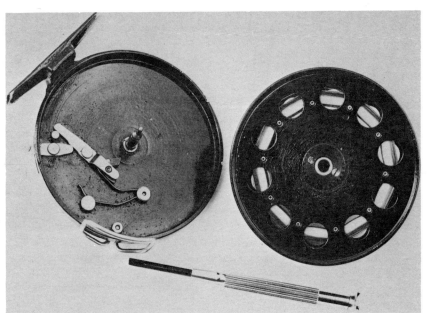

parts of the spinning models, especially where any form of mechanical braking is fitted.

Usually these mechanical brakes involve leather or felt pads running against the rear of the spool; oil on them obviously negates their working capacity, so try to keep them free from any form of lubricant. If, however, they do become loaded then trundle the whole effort round to your local garage, and give the various parts a blast of air from one of their compressed air jets. Most superfluous oil will be blown clear, together with any other gunge and muck that is jammed into inaccessible parts of springs, clips etc.

Our final category of centrepins contains those that are used for sea fishing, which almost invariably means boatwork. Originally these reels were made of wood (as, indeed were many of the freshwater varieties) beautifully turned out of walnut or mahogany and lavishly fitted out with brass furnishings. There were two basic types – the Nottingham, which consisted of a drum that fitted into a turned wooden back which housed the check mechanism, and the Scarborough type with the drum fitting directly on the spindle which in turn was held by a brass flange that housed the reel saddle. Many of these golden oldies are still giving yeoman service; others are rapidly becoming collectors' items.

Wooden reels require stripping and re-varnishing at regular intervals (rather in the manner of wooden rods) although the inside of the Nottingham reel backplate should never be varnished. Instead, it should be liberally and repeatedly coated with boot polish applied with a boot brush until the whole is soaked and completely impervious to the action of water. Treated in this way there can be no fear of the wood swelling and jamming when fishing. Apart from a little regular oiling and a burnish round the brightwork (a labour of love in our reckoning) these reels will go on literally forever.

More modern centrepin sea reels include the Alvey range, which consist of a one-piece metal backplate with a wooden – or, more recently, a plastic – spool. These Australian imports are rugged, hard-wearing and need the minimum of maintenance. A refinement we particularly like in this range is a small felt pad mounted in the spindle hole on each handle, ensuring that a constant film of oil can filter down on to this hardwearing area.

In the big game range there are stainless steel models, and a few old Bakelite reels that are first-rate until dropped! This, incidentally, is the most devastating thing that can happen to a centrepin of any sort. If they land on one edge, there is a chance that either a handle, or worse still, part of the rim of the spool will snap off or badly buckle.

Handles can usually be re-fixed with bigger screws and Araldite glue. Even the broken rim is repairable – Photo 26 shows just such damage, and how it has been repaired by means of a metal plate screwed and glued into place to hold the rim firmly. This type of repair gives the reel a further lease of useful life.

MULTIPLIERS

When we evaluated various multiplying reels in our book, *Spinners, Spoons and Wobbled Baits*, we reckoned that although one paid a high price for a multiplier, the investment was invariably well repaid by the degree of engineering that went into each model. Our experience, together with that of

28 Six-monthly strip-down of a freshwater multiplying reel. In the foreground, the oil-bottle and spares supplied with the reel.

29 Checking the spindle ends against the light for signs of distortion.

30 Gearing on the spreader-mechanism. Often missed by the oil-bottle and a source of wear and trouble when it is.

thousands of other anglers, is that given a little regular maintenance they carry on for years. In fact, most multipliers tend to
develop their faults only after the first attempt by the 'nail-file
and pliers' brigade, who take them apart to see what makes them
tick.

We said earlier that it is impossible to give the maintenance
directions for every type of reel on the market, so we must content ourselves here with routine maintenance in general, which
obviously must be modified by the directions contained in the
manufacturers' handbooks.

Most multipliers are fitted with external oil and grease points,
and these should be used at regular intervals. Stripping is only
necessary once every season, or when the reel has become soaking wet. More especially this matters if the reel has been dropped
directly into the water or on a bank, where mud and grit can
enter into the works. Stripping, in most cases, is accomplished
by removing several screws on the outer face at the handle side
of the reel, which will free the gear mechanism, together with
the handles, in one piece. This can be laid aside, and the spool
itself withdrawn, leaving the backplate with its check mechanism, supports and line spreader (where one is fitted) intact.

The exposed parts of the reel can now be dried and cleaned
with a dry cloth, and a little oil sparingly applied on bearing
surfaces only. Make sure that the spreader, and the gear track
that it runs along, is completely clear of dirt – this is a natural
'trapping' place for it, and more reels have been returned as
'faulty' to the manufacturers with a blockage in this department
than bears thinking about!

Whilst the spool is free of the backplate it is as well to check
the spindles for distortion. This distortion, which amounts to
bending of the spindle ends where they house into the respective
bushes at the front and rear plates, occurs quite frequently and
often remains unnoticed for a long period whilst the angler
plays with the drag adjustment, braking mechanism, etc. in an
attempt to cure erratic casting, until eventually either the reel is
sold, or discreetly left on one side. It invariably occurs when the
angler over-strains the spool by pulling hard on a hooked obstruction – rarely, if ever, by playing an extra large fish.

The quickest check for this fault is to hold the spool vertically
in front of the eye and against a light background, in a good light,

31 Ensure that the weights are in place on the governing mechanism before re-assembly.

slowly revolve the spool until it is completely examined, then to reverse it to check the spindle at the other end. Distortion will immediately be seen, and a new spool should be replaced into the body of the reel *before* it is used again. Failure to do this will result in damage to the bearings in which the spindles run – and added expense and inconvenience whilst the reel is returned for professional attention.

Another problem that affects the spool is over-tightening of nylon monofilament line, caused by constant re-spooling under extreme pressure (again, pulling against an underwater obstruction). Nylon has an elastic effect, and over-tightness can produce such pressure that it will crush the whole spool quite easily. The answer is occasionally to unwind the line off the spool and then re-wind it with gentle pressure, or to use an all-metal spool – providing that one has been made available for the type of reel that you are using.

Once the spool and its supporting items have been checked, the reel can be re-assembled. Drop the spool into the backplate, having greased the check mechanism and lubricated the end

32 A sea multiplying reel stripped to allow corrosion to be cleared from under the reel saddle, inside the back plate, etc.

bearing on that side. Then ensure that the governing mechanism – especially the counter weights – are in position (where fitted), lubricate the spindle end and re-locate the handle assembly. To help in stripping the reel when next it has to be done, dip the end of each securing bolt in a little grease before tightening down.

Our last thoughts on multipliers concern adjustment of the various tension points that are supplied to assist in preventing an overrun. Caution on the part of the angler and a natural desire to prevent the dreaded 'bird's nest' appearing usually results in these adjustments being bolted-up tight immediately after the reel has been purchased. In many cases they are never released again, and this means wear – and lots of it – more especially where the end-play adjustment knob is bolted hard on the spindle end. By all means use that initial caution when first operating the reel. But do remember that the manufacturers supply a guide to tensioning with their handbook that accompanies the reel – and revert to this as soon as possible.

The final paragraph on this section on reel maintenance is

33 Some of the complicated mechanism inside a centrepin spinning reel – in this case a Hardy's Silex. Briefly, oil should be kept to a minimum on the moving parts, whilst thin grease should be used on the centre spindle.

cautionary. Working with lighter fuel (petrol) and some of the freeing agents used to ease awkward screws and nuts out of place can be dangerous, because the fluids are highly inflammable. Obviously, smoking and naked lights should be guarded against, and ideally, the job best done in a shed or small room which can be well ventilated, apart from the rest of the home.

Floats

INTRODUCTION

Any young angler examining the great range of floats available in the tackle shops of today may be forgiven for taking good floats for granted. He is unlikely to be aware of the great revolution that has taken place in float making and the reasons for it. Since some of these reasons are fundamental to float design it is as well to preface the following sections with a brief summary of them. The current variety of floats is due to the great upsurge of interest in match fishing that began about a decade ago, but the story really begins somewhat before that. Prior to 1965, although a considerable variety of materials had been used in float making, the most common materials had been bird quills, cork, wood (including cane) and balsa. Sometimes paper, celluloid, bone and metal were involved. After 1965 various plastics were used much more commonly, and today a huge variety of materials is used, and can be used by the amateur.

Just before the rise of match fishing really got underway and the demand for numerous, well finished, shot-marked floats reached a peak, there was a big debate in the angling newspapers and magazines on the principles of float making. To a certain extent this was reflected in several float-making competitions run by the magazines, but the centre of the debate began with an article published in the now extinct magazine *Fishing* for 5 June 1964 and entitled 'Float design fallacies'. Its author, Dr Terry Coulson, is a physicist. He followed that first article with others over the period 1964 to 1966 in which he set down the scientific principles of float behaviour, dealing with such topical subjects as buoyancy, streamlining, float materials, antennae and so on. Although setting down the scientific facts in a completely uncompromising manner he made no attempt to dissuade anglers from using their 'favourite' float or method, maintaining that personal feeling and enjoyment was highly important. He did, however, by implication suggest that anglers should refrain from giving false scientific arguments to support their concepts of the ideal float for this and that situation.

The articles in *Fishing* were accompanied by a lively debate in the Opinion column of the same journal and several famous (and skilled) anglers succumbed to Coulson's grasp of the facts and his logical and reasonable use of them. It is, in our opinion, no coincidence that this period was immediately followed by several firms producing a whole series of well-designed, well-finished floats. Never before had such a variety been available to the angler, and a major contributory factor was the demand by match anglers for precision built floats: whereas to a specimen hunter the weight-carrying capacity may not matter to the odd BB, to a matchman a dust shot can make the difference between total failure and success.

As a matter of fact Coulson went on to compare swing tips, butt indicators, 'dough' bobbins and other bite indicators, all from the standpoint of sensitivity and efficiency. Again he did not insist that anglers use the most efficient method; in his view, if an angler uses an inefficient system because he enjoys it, then he knows what he is doing! Anglers will almost always refuse to face the facts though they stare them in the face, and nowhere so spectacularly as in float fishing.

Let us offer some examples. Many anglers maintain that a streamlined body should be pointed into the water through which it will travel when moved by a fish: pointed downwards, rounded upwards if you like, as in a *Fishing Gazette* pike bung. This is quite incorrect. Given two *F.G.* bungs of the same size, the one rounded end upwards, the other rounded end downwards, it is the *second* which is streamlined and causes less resistance on the take. Without going into the physics involved, consider the leading edge of an aeroplane wing: it is *rounded* into the wind and much less rounded at the back edge. Only at supersonic speeds does this principle of streamlining change, and even a mad zander or carp run is not likely to reach such limits! Therefore, whether you are making pike floats or a balsa bodied antenna, if you want maximum streamlining (other things being equal) any bulge should be downwards. You see this very precisely illustrated in the example of Billy Lane's Trent Trotter Float. Even the great man made mistakes, however, as when he described his new Zoomer as more streamlined than the old style Zoomer (*Float Fishing* Fig. 13): it is, in fact, less streamlined.

Another misconception concerns the antennae on the various very popular antennae floats. Many anglers still think that if the antenna is made of very light material then the fish will have to give a lesser pull to dip it than if the antenna was of heavier material. In fact, if the floats are of the same size and the antennae of the same diameter and length, the pull required is exactly the same even if the material of one is, say, aluminium tube, and the other peacock quill. The way to get less resistance on the pull is to use a *finer* antenna such as a plastic bristle or a fine sliver of cane, a thing to bear in mind when building antennae out of Sarkandas reed.

One of the commonest errors surrounds long distance float casting. We used to believe, along with most other anglers, that if you used a heavy float carrying say three swan shots such that the addition of a single BB would sink it, then this was just as sensitive to the bite as a float carrying one BB when the addition of one BB would sink it. Therefore we used the heavy floats for long range casting for small fish, shotted down so that only a short length was visible. This is nonsense. The way Coulson demonstrated this was to imagine a length of broom handle shotted so that the addition of one BB would sink it! Looked at like this it is clear that our ideas were all wrong. Because a large, heavy object has considerable inertia a fair old pull would be required to dip it as quickly as the dip of a small float. That dream demolished, it means one should always use the smallest float possible for the circumstances: or, put another way, the largest you can get away with. Just as you would use the smallest possible lead for ledgering, in fact.

It is not our intention here to go into the science in detail. Anyone wishing to do that could consult *Fishing* Nos. 68–71 for 1964 and subsequent articles over the following two years. They will find enough science and good sense to keep them happy for a long while. Today we may have gone overboard a little in the variety of floats available; producing innumerable types that seem fundamentally very little different, at least to our eyes. Design and usage errors are also beginning to creep in again.

Billy Lane has pointed to one such error resulting from anglers having crazes; for example, fishing the waggler float in still-waters. The waggler, essentially a peacock quill, was used because the material carries a fair shot load, and at least some of it drags the bottom. When fishing a lake or small, sluggish river there is no point in using heavier weights unless you want distance, and in that case there are better casters than wagglers. Wagglers are used in a kind of combination of stret pegging and trotting, with the bait and some shot on the bottom, preferably under conditions of some flow and, in Billy Lane's view, ideally with a downstream wind and turbulence.

It seems that every float that is newly designed, catches on, becomes a craze, and is used in all manner of unsuitable situations; but if the angler remembers some of the above points, and any made in the following sections, we hope he will not go too far wrong and will not submerge under the weight of scientific argument.

DIFFERENT TYPES OF FLOATS

It will be clear from our introduction that there are probably fewer *basic* types of floats than there are named floats on the market. This is not to criticise these named floats in any way. And to classify floats, as roughly as we propose to do, is not to say that one particular float does not have several different uses in different circumstances. Anglers *do* classify floats. For example, both Ivan Marks and Bill Watson have described duckers as little more than reversed Avon floats. Both duckers and Avons have a body on a straight stem; in the former the body is low down so that the stem acts as an antenna; in the latter the body is high up so the stem acts as a keel of sorts. We are about to list a number of popular modern floats in a small number of categories: within these categories they do a variety of jobs, such as close range work, stret pegging, acting as sliders and so on, but the list gives some idea of the limited *basic* pattern within which we experiment. In other words the grouping does not classify floats strictly as to detailed use. This will be considered in particular cases in later sections. Use of tackle is strictly outside the scope of this book, and for use of floats the reader is strongly referred to books by Billy Lane and Ivan Marks.

Avon floats Traditionally these had a cork, wooden or celluloid body on a straight stem, the body being towards the top of the stem. Today the body is usually balsa. They are stable floats, good load carriers, and they ride flowing and turbulent water well and in a largely upright position: standard Avons; perch or grayling bobbers; Billy Lane Chubber; Ivan Marks' Pacemaker; fluted Avons.

Antennas Most modern floats fall into this category. The idea of an antenna float is that the body, usually of balsa, is deeply sunk below the surface and the surface is reached by an antenna of relatively thinner material (plastic bristle, peacock quill, cane spine, Sarkandas reed). This way the float is held stable in the wind. More commonly than Avons they are used in slow and stillwater, often in deep water as sliders, or attached bottom end only: Duckers; Darts; Wagglers with antennae; reverse crow, swan quill, etc.; Onion; Missile; Mini Missile; Zoomer; Canal Antennae (Billy Lane); Swinger; Sarkandas Peacock antenna; Super Missile etc.

'Quills' As Bill Watson and others have so rightly said, stick floats are merely a modern equivalent of the old fashioned bird quill. Quills are interesting in that they can be used, in their various weights, lengths and sizes, in almost all the circumstances that can the Avons and Antennas, and in a sense therefore they are more versatile whilst occasionally lacking the specialist application: pheasant, crow, swan quill, etc.; porcupine quill; stick; wire-stemmed stick; straight balsa; peacock quill; Waggler (without antenna).

Quite a lot of floats remain unmentioned, but most will fit easily into this scheme of things. There are exceptions. For example, Trent Trotters and Trout Trotters are roughly midway between Avons and Antennas, whilst Ivan Marks' Carrot is midway between a 'quill' and an Antenna. Some of the floats omitted are commercially made plastic or metal jobs and, unlike all the above, cannot be made easily by the amateur.

MATERIALS AND TOOLS

There is no end to the amount and variety of materials that are useful, and the same really applies to tools. Thus we have all sorts of plastic, wood, canes, quills, paints, varnishes, sealers, etc. But a basic list of float materials must include the following: bird feather quills (swan, crow, pheasant and others for experimental purposes); porcupine quills; peacock quills; balsa wood; cane spine; softwood dowel; elder pith; Sarkandas reed; and cork. However, it is possible to gather all manner of materials which are useful at times, such as sheets of thin plastic (for vanes); polystyrene (for visibility bobs); plastic drinking straws; aluminium and brass tubing; various grades and types of wire; fibre glass (as in solid glass spinning rods, or thin, hollow end pieces). It is possible, obviously, to gather many of these items oneself, such as bird quills and elder pith, and many others can be 'acquired' on one's travels. It is exactly the same mental attitude that is needed for tying one's own flies: eyes open, and acquisitiveness.

The same rules apply to tools, and the more you have the more you can do – and with greater ease. Again we draw the line at a lathe, for few anglers will have them: various machines used by professionals such as Les Beecroft (lathes, dipping machines, etc.) are for producing a large number of floats, some at least of which will be supplied to other anglers if not actually sold. Our purpose is to make a few of each type of float, or to invent new ones, and for this almost everything can be done by hand. As a matter of fact an ordinary hand drill can be used as a primitive lathe if clamped to a work bench, and probably this is as much as we shall need. Such a system was recently illustrated by Bill Watson in his superb book *Floatmakers' Manual*, but a number of versions have been seen over the years. Of course, if you can cadge time on a friend's lathe, then so much the better. A few years ago, with the assistance of such a friend, Barrie made a very long, thin drill bit specially designed for cutting long straight holes through plug and float bodies.

With many float-making materials, such as balsa, it is not always necessary to use a drill when you can lay your hands on a cork-boring set. These are sharpened tubes of different diameters, each with a little handle, and they can be used to cut reasonable holes in most materials softer than beech or obeche wood (the latter being the softest known hardwood!). If it *is* necessary to use a drill in float making *always* penetrate the material slowly with frequent pauses for cooling. This way you suffer less frustration from damaged float parts.

In addition you will need penknives, Stanley knives, rasps, razor blades, sandpapers in various grades, wet and dry grinding paper or emery cloth, a vice, hacksaws, wire cutters, various drill bits, and numerous glues, fillers, sealers, paints and varnishes. In short, anything you can lay your hands on.

Storage is no great problem if supplies of cane spines, quills, in fact anything elongate – including tools – are conveniently contained in a set of variously sized tins mounted on a board. Glue the tins to the board, tall at the back, smallest to the front, and then paint the whole assembly a suitable colour. Very simple and almost too obvious, but the advantages soon become clear as you memorise the positions of the various materials you will be working with.

CANE

The Chinese sometimes use thin whole cane, in various lengths. Some look like stick floats and others are used in long strings of 1 in. pieces to which a new length is added if more buoyancy is required. In this last case the nature of the bite is deduced from the number of lengths which submerge and their manner of doing so. But in this country cane is usually used as cane spine (that is, split bamboo smoothed and sanded to dowel-like rods of various thicknesses) in Antennas and as stems for Avon floats. It is easy enough to split your own bamboo: simply use a blunt knife and tap this with a wooden mallet so that it splits along the fibres. Bamboo can be bought in quantity from most good tackle shops and this is certainly the most convenient way to get it. It takes out all the slog of sanding down your split slivers. Cane can be used as the stem of stick floats, Duckers, or as the antennae on Darts, Wagglers or on general Antennas.

PLASTIC

Various bristles are useful for Antennae, particularly polypropylene bristles. You will remember from the introduction that for a given length the narrower diameter antenna requires less to pull it under, and fine bristles are therefore excellent as antennas. With distance, visibility becomes a problem and then a sight bob (of peacock quill or polystyrene) can be glued on the top. We use exactly the same system with antenna-bearing pike floats, although there sensitivity is usually less important. Plastic drinking straws can be incorporated in floats either as antennas or as floats in their own right (as can rolled paper or plastic sheet) but we can find no use that cannot be achieved by other stronger materials. Barrie has used fibre glass (perhaps not really to be considered under this heading) in exactly the same way as polypropylene bristle, but generally prefers the latter.

CORK

We do not use cork nowadays for floats, though we remember the pleasure of working with fine-grained corks when building grayling floats or big Avons. Today, balsa would be our first choice.

PEACOCK QUILLS

There was panic buying of these a few years ago when the supply of quills from the Far East seemed likely to be stopped by conservationists-cum-nationalists. We built up a fair stock, for it is one of the best float-making materials there is, either when used as an antenna, a body (as in some Wagglers), or directly as a piece of peacock quill. The Taylor brothers made famous the use of peacock quill with the lift method in tench fishing. The piece of quill itself was left unpainted and was trimmed on the day, as appropriate, with a pair of scissors. It was attached bottom end only by means of a float rubber. When Barrie used the system, either with the lift method or with float ledgering and sliding lead, he bound the bottom of the floats tightly with thread to give a tapered purchase for the float rubber – and found this much more efficient. Peacock quills are much more easily worked free of their herl than swan or goose quills but are otherwise rather softer and more prone to leaking where the pith lies under the thinnest part of the skin. This, at least, was Barrie's experience, though not shared by his friends. (Could they be better workmen?)

BALSA

This is beautiful material to work with and we wonder what the float making industry would do without it! Although rather soft, when sealed and painted it is indestructible in reasonable circumstances. It can be bored by needles, or drilled, and is very easy to work with a Stanley knife and sandpaper. We usually give finished surfaces two coats of sealer before a final fine sanding and painting.

If you obtain balsa rods in square cross-section they have to be carefully worked down with a blade (taking off the corners) before work with coarse sandpaper can begin. We much prefer to buy round dowel, from which we find it easier to get the right tapers to a float body. We make the hole through the body at an early stage, and usually keep a spare cane spine (or needle) through it whilst working; this enables the float to be put in the hand drill chuck and the sandpaper worked under the balsa as it turns. It is essential that there is no wobble of the rotating axis.

ELDER PITH

Barrie remembers buying elder pith bodied Avons from Tom Watson of Nottingham, and beautiful floats they were. Then he made up some himself from bought bodies, and finally produced his own pith. The trick is to go out in winter when the dead stems can be easily seen. Pick the biggest, dead, straight stems and then split the bark with a knife. At this time it is usually quite easy to take out the pith, whereas in summer it often sticks to the wall of tube in which it grows. It is very very soft, difficult to work with the finest sandpaper, and boring it can be tricky. The enthusiastic float maker can really only be happy when he has a coat of sealer and paint on it. Then it becomes a good load carrier and the basis of a fine Avon float. It keeps really well if kept dry and straight.

SARKANDAS REED

A 'new' material this, with a mixed reputation but in widespread use. As pointed out by Billy Lane some years ago, the outer shell does not take paint easily unless roughed up first. B.L. does this in a lathe and Bill Watson in his own Sarkandas reed mill, but we use sandpaper simply because we make a fewer number of floats. It takes quite a long time to sand down properly half a dozen good reeds. When cutting this reed you need a very sharp blade: work all round cutting through the skin, or cut at least deeply scoring it, then snap.

QUILLS AND QUILL FLOATS

Before the clamour for scientific floats with calculated displacement, wind resistance, and shot capacities took place, there were two sorts of float. One was the quill – the other the quill with a cork body. We began our fishing with them, and lived with and swore by them as guaranteed to show the slightest knock; in fact we possess, make and use some of them to this day.

Mind you, today's shop-bought quill is a mighty sight different in price than in our young days. Then a quill – a good, hefty goose quill – cost sixpence ($2\frac{1}{2}$ new pence), whilst a cork-on-quill, a round-bodied perch bobber coloured with red and green paint, needing a long string of shot to cock it, cost a shilling (5 new pence).

Quills that lend themselves to easy float making, roughly in their order of size, are those of the swan, turkey, goose, crow, duck and pheasant. The quill from the porcupine is also excellent, but the chances of obtaining them other than at a tackle shop, ready-made, are remote. There are one or two zoos that used to sell them on their souvenir stand to visitors, but whether this is still so we do not know. They can also be 'lifted' from some zoo pens when the animals have finished with them!

Possible sources of supply for the birds' quills we have listed are poultry dealers (where most make an appearance at some time of year or other), local gamekeepers, and farms. The most difficult quills to obtain are those of the swan, and a suggestion for a possible source here is a park-keeper where the birds are kept on an ornamental lake. Ken has also had success with the local R.S.P.C.A. Inspector – albeit with a touch of conscience; the last two bundles he obtained were from birds killed through nylon line left by anglers.

The only tool necessary for preparing a quill is a sharp safety razor blade, together with some fine fly-tying silk for whipping end rings, and some copal varnish. Select a quill, and with slow, steady strokes cut free the fibres from either side, taking care to cut as closely to the body of the quill as possible, without actually puncturing it. Once stripped, the float can be trimmed to length, and the end fastening prepared.

If you examine a quill closely, you will see that at its thinnest end, on the inside of the natural curve that the stalk possesses, there is a soft pith-type formation. This can be cut through easily with the razor blade at a point approximately $\frac{3}{4}$ in. from the end, until the hard bark of the quill itself is felt below the blade – and once this point is reached the cutting action should stop. Now turn the quill on its side, and make a long cut through the soft pith from the cross-cut made earlier to the end of the quill itself. This will free the pith, and leave a long thin flap attached to the quill that can be folded back to the main body.

Leave a small gap through which line from the reel can be run (Photos. 34–5) and then whip the flap against the main body, and smear the joint with varnish. An alternative is to fold this flap back over a small ring through which the line will run – the rings are quite easily made from ladies' wire hairpins, or even wire paperclips, bent and cut to shape. Some very long quills are better with a whipping along the bottom end to strengthen them – an easy task, and shown in Photo. 35.

Of course, porcupine quills do not need trimming except sometimes to clip off a dangerously sharpened end. Instead, a U-shaped piece of wire with a bulb at the end is bent into shape, and then whipped at the thin (most tapered) end of the quill. Once this end ring is secured, then the quill will be ready for painting. A complete body colour is unnecessary – just the tip that will protrude above the water, plus a little below the surface. Using a rough piece of cloth, work over this part of the quill until all signs of the natural oil that encases it are removed. Now open the tin of paint that is to be used, dip the end inch

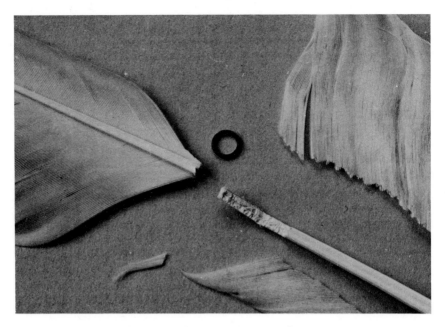

34 Preparation of the base of the quill for the float shown in Photo. 35.

or so of the float into this (less, of course, if the float is a small one) and allow the surplus to drip off. Hang the float to dry with the wet end downwards, over an old newspaper.

Further colours can be superimposed by dipping the float, say half an inch, into the new paint after the first coat is dry. The advantage of this dipping as opposed to painting method is that sharp, clear-cut lines all round the float will be formed, plus a good even covering, and all in one operation. Colours used are a matter of choice, but yellow and red tips, with a white backing band, take a lot of beating. Finally, when all is dry, the float will benefit from a coat of copal varnish that acts as a protection against possible leaking into the hollow body of the quill itself.

One of the problems with quills is getting them straight. Crow and pheasant do not need straightening but swan quills may do: a straightened, reversed swan quill is a superb float, streamlined correctly (as outlined above), almost antenna-like, and a good load carrier, so it is well worth any trouble in the making. Having removed the herl, and this is not always as easy as we make it sound, boil the quill in water liberally dosed with

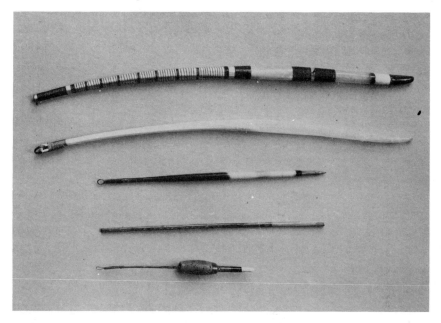

35 Various types of homemade quill floats.

bicarbonate of soda. (Incidentally, when cutting off the herl, you should remember always to cut *with* the lie of the herl, not against it, since the latter method more easily cuts through the outer skin of the feather – as does peeling off the herl with the fingers.) Eventually the quill will soften in the solution, and on removal from the water it should be taped down firmly to a length of 1 in. square wood. The quill always curves towards the pithy side, so tape it upwards or downwards, not to the side.

When the quill has dried it *should* be straight, but we offer no guarantees! It is tempting at this stage to use a little very fine sandpaper to try to smooth off the herl bases since these never come away as smoothly as one would wish. But you will find that the herl bases come off a little more easily if the quill is first treated to a layer of varnish or sanding sealer, and *then* lightly sandpapered.

This method of quill straightening does not work too well with porcupine quills, which really need heat treatment. Revolve them over a gas ring and with practice you can straighten them without burning them. Wearing old gloves may prevent burning yourself with the hot quill, but make it difficult to judge whether the quill is hot enough to straighten. Only trial will tell. Perhaps it is best to use only straight quills in the first place!

There is another way of straightening swan quills which results in one of the most beautiful floats (Photo. 38) and this is by cutting the straightest clear end of two different quills and then splicing the two together. Care must be taken to choose one that is fractionally smaller than the other so that it pushes firmly into the larger one for glueing and whipping. The float then has a fat end of clear quill, and a thin end, also of clear quill, and can be fished reverse quill or the 'right' way up.

All quills can be dyed in Dylon dyes, and we prefer a dark green, brown or black. These dyes have a nice matt finish too, but in floats a matt finish can be a mixed blessing. Certainly it is more pleasing to the eye than a glossy float, but a float with a *very* smooth surface has rather less resistance as it slides under on the bite! What we need is a dull, smooth finish, which really means preparing the surface well before further treatment. You can always finish off with a matt varnish over all except the tip of the float.

AVON FLOATS

It is not our intention to describe the making of all the floats listed earlier, but rather to outline the basic construction of a few which involve most of the tricks you need. Bird and porcupine quills have already been dealt with, and of balsa-bodied types the old Avon takes a lot of beating.

The first job is to pick the balsa dowel size and the cane stem size and then, with a knitting needle, run a hole right through the length of the balsa. If you are intending to fit an antenna, use a blunt-ended rod to do this, since a blunt-ended antenna pushed into a blunt-ended hole seems to hold more firmly. But for the Avon the stem needs to go right through.

In smaller Avons a parallel-sided spine of cane can be used. Push it through, perhaps smearing a little glue on it, and then shape the balsa body with blade and sandpaper. If using the hand drill it would be better to use a false stem until the body is completed. With large Avons, say carrying several swan shots, it is

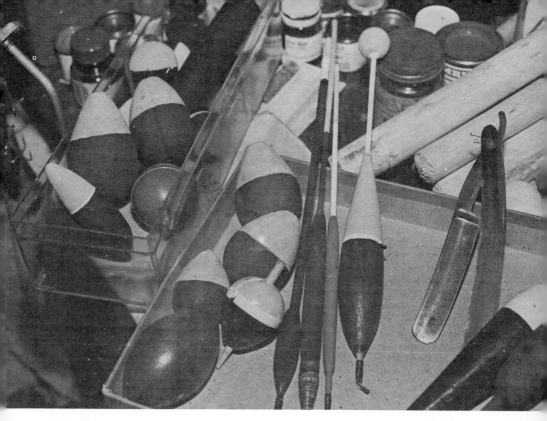

36 Various antenna floats, leaded zoomers, pike floats and float making equipment.

nicer if the cane stem itself is tapered and inserted point end downwards. You can buy tapered cane stems in various sizes but it is quite easy to taper one yourself. Other dowel materials can be used instead of cane, and it is quite reasonable to make Avons with peacock quill, swan quill, or Sarkandas reed stems. Whip over the contact of body and stem; treat the whole lot with sanding sealer or thinned Durafix, and then sand again gently before painting. If you like a nice dark, dull finish to the main body and lower stem the whole thing can be dropped in hot Dylon, but we prefer to paint cane. When it comes to painting the tip we recommend using a brilliant white undercoat, getting this right first before putting on the fire orange, red or whatever takes your fancy. As a matter of fact we always put too long a length of brightly coloured tip. On the accompanying photographs (Photos. 36–38) the coloured portion would be better half the length or less, at least on some of the floats.

37 The tackle maker's bench.

The same photographs, incidentally, show several different types of Avons: cork bodied, celluloid with bone inserts, and balsa on cane. There is certainly great scope for variation. For example, quite a few anglers have the stem in two parts; the lower, longer stem of cane and the upper (above water) part of Sarkandas reed or peacock quill, but the advantages gained (fractionally more rapid cocking with the heavier cane below) seem to us not worth the trouble. But by all means experiment.

So far nothing has been said about fixing the eye at the bottom of the float. We use fine wire, wrapped round a metal spine so as to get as tiny a hole as is practicable, and then whipped into place with very fine thread. We do not like shrink tubes as a way of holding the eye, since to us they look bulky and ugly. Of course, it is possible to buy very good float eyes from the tackle shops and these are to be recommended. Avon floats are one of the easiest to fish with a rubber at each end, but we usually whip on an eye in case we wish to fish it attached at the bottom end only, or even as a slider.

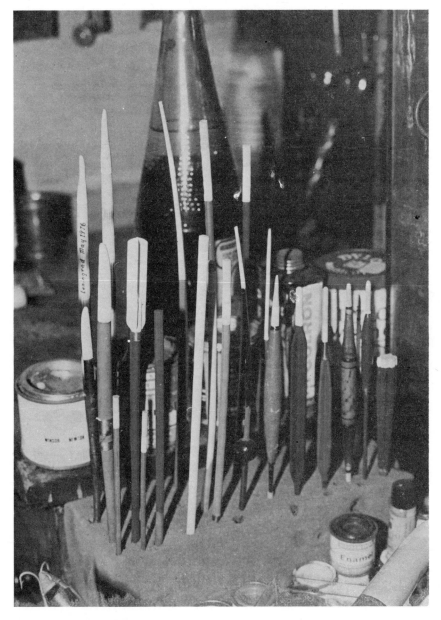

38 Porcupine quills, goose quills, peacock quills, Avons, fluted Avons, cork with celluloid and bone: the final tip colour is yet to be added.

ANTENNA FLOATS

Once again these come in many varieties. In this example the balsa body is prepared as in the Avon and a 12 in. length of polypropylene bristle is cut and fitted with a sight bob made of a $\frac{1}{2}$ in. length of peacock quill with its edges rounded a little. The tip of the bristle is smeared with glue and pushed almost through the length of quill. The balsa body has a fine enough needle pushed through it and then, from the bottom end, is drilled out for about half its length to take a Sarkandas reed insert. The top of the length of Sarkandas reed is speared for about a $\frac{1}{2}$ in. so that it will take the bristle spine (or fibre glass if you prefer it). Push the bristle right through the balsa body, glue and locate it in the piece of reed, then push *this* back into the balsa body after smearing it with glue. Allow the whole thing to dry and then with fine sandpaper smooth off any rough parts, edges, or surplus glue. Glue a ring into the base of the Sarkandas reed and liberally cover the base with Araldite. All that remains now is to seal and paint. Other floats are constructed in a basically similar fashion, for example Zoomers and Missiles, the last with its now famous brass insert.

WAGGLERS

As with stick floats (see below) we may be too finickity about what goes into these floats. After all, as Bill Watson has so succinctly put it, a single length of peacock or Sarkandas will make a good waggler! However, the usual system is to use a fattish body with a short cane insert at the base and a longer (even antenna-like) insert at the top. You can use a peacock quill body and cane upper insert (the easiest combination); a balsa body with peacock insert; or a Sarkandas reed body with a peacock insert. In each case the greatest care should be taken to spike or drill out the body for an inch or two before pushing in the *glued in* glue-smeared insert. In fact, the insert should be pushed in dry to ensure it is dead straight. We think all junctions of inserts and bodies should be smeared with a little extra Araldite and then whipped if possible. Finally, ring and paint in the usual way.

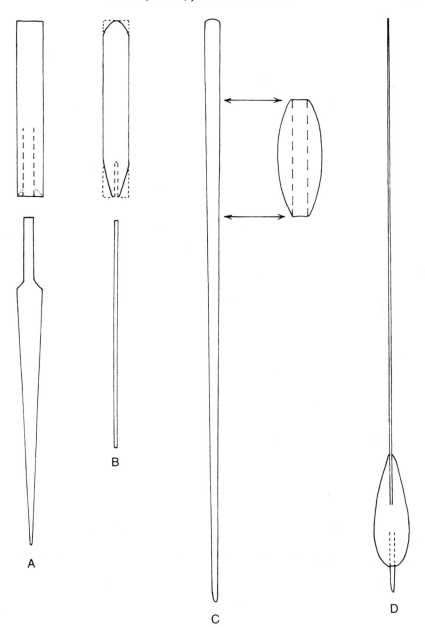

Fig. **B** A & B: stick floats, respectively with balsa top and beech stem, and with balsa top and wire stem. C: basic Avon float construction; the hole through the body should be made a tight fit and loosened gradually. D: basic antenna float pattern, with fibre glass spine as antenna, balsa body and cane basal insert.

STICK FLOATS

Stick floats come in two basic types, those with a cane stem below and a balsa top, and those with a piano wire stem below and a balsa top. With a cane and balsa stick constructed as in Fig. **B**, that is, with just about half the 6 in. length being cane, the float is very nearly self cocking; and with wire stemmed sticks, as figured, the length of piano wire used should have just about the same effect. The overall size of the floats determines the amount of shot carried, but they can be built to carry anything from a few no. 6s to 8 BBs. Many anglers consider the wire stick float better for use in turbulent water, and just as good as the cane and balsa stick in quieter water. To be quite honest, we cannot explain why this should be so – unless anglers are trying to get away with too small a cane and balsa stick in turbulent water. No doubt there are some good technical reasons, but for the moment they elude us. We prefer the wire stick floats anyway!

It would be purposeless to go on describing the basic construction of floats because the techniques briefly outlined will enable you to construct most varieties. If you can make them, then you can design and invent new ones – and we are prepared to bet that they all fall into the same basic scheme we have outlined.

Leads

LEAD MAKING AND ANTI-KINK DEVICES

The decision whether to make one's own leads revolves entirely around economics. Some things are not worth the time and effort to produce – split shot is an instance – whilst other items can present an appreciable saving if the angler can do it himself. Largely, of course, the sea angler will fall into the latter category, for in his branch of the sport loss of end tackle can be high. Of course, one's source of lead enters into the argument for and against home production. If you have to purchase it at market price, then things are not quite as worthwhile as when odd pieces can be bartered for on a demolition site.

Split shot we placed in the not-to-bother league, and fresh-water leads follow close after them. As yet there are no professional moulds for small items on the market (although this situation may alter soon after this book goes into print) and the manufacture of a mould, together with the speed with which the items can be produced, makes the whole business uneconomical. One of the best sources of small ledger weights is an assortment of metal nuts from the local scrap yard.

For a matter of pence a large selection of assorted sizes can be obtained, and once they have been cleaned to remove oil and grease these can be used in the same way as a pierced bullet, held by a stop shot, professional ledger stop, or a half-hitched matchstick. They have an added advantage to cheapness in that the size of bore through which the line passes presents absolutely no resistance to a taking fish. Oh yes, we agree on their in-elegant appearance, but when you are fishing a well-snagged weirpool that swallows ledger tackle, elegance matters for little or nothing.

95

39 Perfectly adequate home-made leads, by Mervyn Wilkinson.

A useful form of combined weight and anti-kink device is the fold-over lead, sometimes called the half-moon lead. These can be made from sheet lead usually available (at a price!) at builders' merchants. As purchased, it is usually far too thick to work if effective leads are to be produced. Thinning it down is a simple process – place it between two wooden boards, lay these on a level concrete surface and hammer with a heavy hammer until the lead is thin and pliable. Now search for a supply of assorted circles that can be used for templates – metal coins and buttons from the family button box are possible sources.

Pair the circles off, one large, one smaller that can fit into the centre of its larger counterpart, leaving a reasonable space around its edges. Mark out both with a sharp nail, and then cut around the outside of the larger circle. Fold it neatly in half, and cut out the folded half-circle that will be marked against the straight edge of the lead. Place the cut-out lead between two small pieces of wood, give it a light tap with a hammer to

40 Lead moulds, as described in the text.

straighten it up, and the job is done. Hang on to all off-cuts: they could come in handy for moulding larger leads.

Moulds for heavy leads – 2 oz upwards – can be purchased from tackle dealers. They are made in two halves (Photos. 39 and 40), and leads with a professional finish are easy to produce from them. Moulten lead is nasty stuff to have an accident with and whilst many anglers manage to do this casting in the kitchen, we prefer to do ours in the open or garage away from the family, especially when young lads are itching to help. Ample heat for melting can be obtained from a blow-lamp or camping stove, set on a firm, level surface. It is possible to purchase a proper ladle in which the lead can be melted; failing this an old, heavy saucepan is ideal – preferably one with a pouring lip.

Whilst the lead is melting, prepare the mould by holding the inside of each section over the flame of a candle until the surface is completely blackened. This coating will help prevent the lead from sticking to the mould itself. Once coated, both halves must be heated to rid them of any trace of moisture – contact with which will cause the lead to spit violently in every direction, bringing some pretty nasty burns.

Now a short length of copper wire is cut and folded into a loop which will fit into the holes set into the mould for this purpose (Photo. 40). Fit both halves of the mould together, and clamp them in a vice; if no vice is available, then the halves must be fastened together with a twist of wire around the body until they are firmly joined. With the pouring hole upwards, gently pour in the lead. Wait a few minutes for the lead to cool, and the mould can be opened and the cast lead released, any small flakes of lead around the joins, pouring hole, etc. filed or snapped off, and the job is done.

As casting progresses and the mould warms up, the job becomes easier, but the hot mould becomes more difficult to grasp with bare fingers. We wear a pair of old leather gloves all the time we are casting, and these protect our hands not only from the heat of the mould, but from any odd splashes that may occur – and often do!

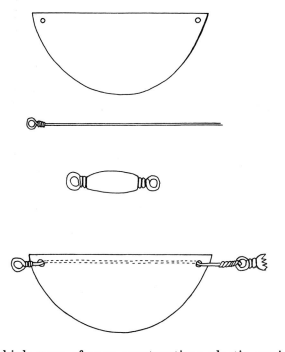

Fig. C Anti-kink vane of easy construction: plastic semicircle and either piano wire or Alasticum wire which should be tight-fitting and have a sharp bend through the holes.

Anti-kink vanes are items that need constant replacement in the spinning angler's tackle box. They are easy to make from thin sheet plastic or celluloid. Cut out a D-shaped piece, the straight edge of which is 1–1½ in. long. Bore, or burn with a hot needle, a hole $\frac{1}{10}$ in. from each corner. Next, twist a loop in a length of fine steel wire (see section on making bar spinners on page 231) and thread this through the hole, pulling the loop up against the edge of the vane. Bend the wire through the second hole, straighten it flush against the body and pass the eye of a small swivel over the wire. Now form and twist-lock a second loop, leaving the swivel free to move within it, cut off the excess wire, straighten, and the job is done. Our diagram (Fig. C) shows how easy the job is.

SLOW SINKING LEADS

Buoyant ledgers or slow sinking leads are one of the most under-used, under-estimated items of tackle. Nor are they readily available in tackle shops, but fortunately you can make your

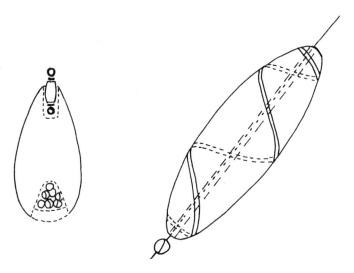

Fig. **D** Slow sinking ledger weights of heavy wood (e.g. greenheart) with, respectively, glued in shot insert in pear-shaped ledger, and spirally wound lead wire (glued in a groove) in fusiform ledger.

own. What they are, in effect, is little more than a plummet, but with less lead so that they sink very slowly. The simplest version is a pear-shaped piece of wood such as greenheart (though any wood will do) with a swivel or ring eye at the top of the pear and a drilled insert filled with lead shot in the bottom half (Fig. **D**). They can also be streamlined with lead wire wrapped around them and sealed in grooves, and can take several other forms as well. But all have one great advantage, namely, great casting weight yet almost no resistance if a fish runs off at an angle and moves the sliding lead a little.

PART TWO

Miscellaneous tackle

Miscellaneous tackle

INTRODUCTION

In Part One we dealt with the major – indeed, the indispensable – items of tackle. In Part Two the problem is more one of selectivity, for here we hope to deal with a variety of the items of miscellaneous equipment with which anglers surround themselves. But because it is in such equipment that the greatest scope for invention lies the problem is not solely one of selectivity; of deciding what to omit and what to include. There are, for example, many different ways in which a handyman coarse fisherman can construct a rod rest: we have selected one particular design because, in our experience, it is the best for most situations. The same principle has been applied to the frames and handles of landing nets, to bait boxes and holdalls.

There are many desirable items which are not included but, as we explained in the introduction to Part One, we are not concerned in entering into competition with tackle dealers. If a commercially manufactured article is in all respects efficient, we use it. The D.I.Y. enthusiast can, if he wishes, buy the component parts of an electric bite alarm and assemble them satisfactorily. In doing so, he may save a little money, but he will not have improved upon the efficiency of the commercial product.

Nor have we dealt with nets, net-making and knots. (The latter, of course, is not strictly tackle and is a specialised subject. See Ken Whitehead's book *Knots for the Angler*.) The trouble with nets is that most (but not all) have been made obsolete by the introduction of micromesh. We have done our share of net-making in the past, and we still have the tools. Today, it is fast becoming a traditional skill so little used as to develop into a folk-art.

Another borderline claimant for inclusion was bite indicators in general, but since these vary so much – from a tiny piece of silver paper to complicated contraptions involving ping pong balls and hair grips – and since for each species there is an equally wide range of methods, most of which do not need 'making' as such, we decided it would be impossible to give representative systems in reasonable space. *Some* bite indicators, such as swing tips, we have illustrated but not described since their construction is so obvious from the illustrations. With such items the only things that vary are length, weight, colour, etc. for particular circumstances.

Most anglers would like to become near-professional at rod making, float making, fly tying, etc. since they will be oft repeated activities. But we have yet to meet an angler so devoted to self-help that he insists on making his own baskets, and since a professionally-made basket may well last half a lifetime there seemed little point in including basket-making as a D.I.Y. activity. Nevertheless, baskets can be repaired and the purchase of a replacement deferred, so a modest entry on basket restoration will be found in the following pages.

Obviously, we cannot explain all the reasons for the inclusions and omissions in this section, but we have given every item full consideration. Of necessity, we offer a personal selection and we certainly do not claim that every item mentioned is an original gem. Many ideas have come from other people and other sources: see, for example, the entries in the bibliography on page 249.

LANDING NET FRAMES

CIRCULAR

The round landing net frame requires access to welding equipment or the aid of a welder. This is no great problem for, as mentioned earlier, there are plenty of professionals around who are generally happy to demonstrate their skills. Failing this, you can take the design to the nearest worker in wrought-iron; he will charge very little for so small a job. Since the landing net frame now described cost £1.50 *in toto* in 1977 – several pounds cheaper than most commercial frames at that time – a small charge for labour is an acceptable overhead.

All you need for this job is an 8 ft length of $\frac{1}{4}$ in. black mild steel, a $\frac{3}{8}$ in. bolt, and some rivets or small nuts and bolts. Your working equipment amounts to no more than a hammer, a hand drill and bits, a vice, a pair of pliers and a pair of gardening gloves.

The length of steel is calculated from the diameter you intend the frame to be; we are assuming, in this example, a diameter of 30 in., which is big enough to land any pike in Britain. Since the circumference of a circle is $2\pi r$, the minimum length you need for a 30 in. diameter frame is $2 \times 3{\cdot}1416 \times 15 = 94\frac{1}{4}$ in. In fact, the metal needs to be in three lengths: say two of 32 in. and one of $32\frac{1}{2}$ in.

Using gloves and pliers to hold the rod (black mild steel is an uncomfortably efficient conductor of heat) heat the end of the longest piece and then tap the end round the anvil end of your vice until you have a ring eye with an internal diameter big enough to take a $\frac{3}{8}$ in. nut comfortably loosely. On one end of the two shorter lengths weld the hexagonal head of the bolt so that it lies at right-angles to the length of rod (Photo. 42).

41 Round landing net, 30 in. diameter, shown in a conveniently folded position.

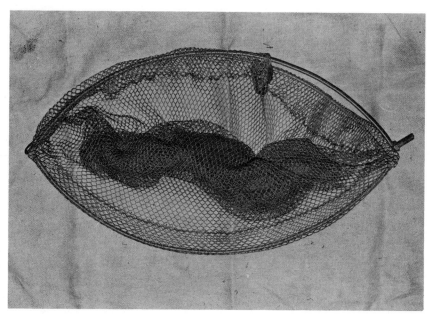

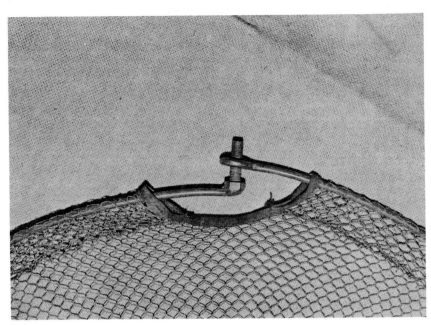

42 Detail of welded bolt and ring eye connector for landing net handle.

43 Detail of simple rivet or small nut and bolt join for folding 30 in. diameter round landing net.

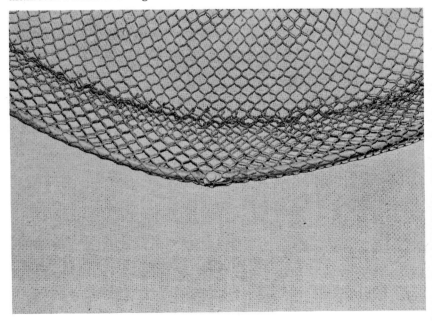

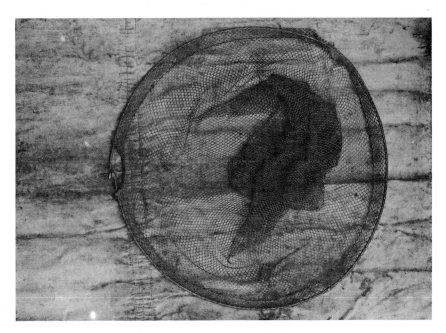

44 Round landing net, 30 in. diameter, in full open position.

The next step is to bend all three pieces so that they fit loosely together to form a circle 30 in. in diameter. This is best done by making a triangular-shaped former out of laths of wood, each side being 26 in. long. Bend the heated rods to the apexes of the former so that its corners lie at the bolt and the two points which will later be riveted. On completion, the three rods should now form a circle and when lying on the floor the welded bolt should lie in the *horizontal plane* pointing away from the circle at 90°. The ring eye should fit over it so that about an inch of the bolt shows; in other words, the ring eye should lie in the *vertical plane*.

The final stage is to tap a flat (when heated) on the ends of each rod where they will be riveted together. When flattened at the ends to $\frac{7}{16}$ in. wide the metal will still be over $\frac{1}{8}$ in. thick in the horizontal plane. Drill holes of about $\frac{1}{8}$-$\frac{3}{16}$ in. diameter in the flats and secure with appropriate rivets (copper) or nuts and bolts: we prefer the latter. With the nuts in position, tap over the ends so that the hinges are stiff but not tight.

What you have made is no second-rate landing net frame.

Indeed, having used a variety of shapes, sizes and designs of frames, commercial and home-made, we maintain that this is without question the best. Of course, the figures quoted above can be modified should you wish to have a smaller-framed net. Incidentally, the frame does not rust; with the net constantly rubbing its surface it takes on a polished brown appearance which is most pleasing.

SPRINT RIM

These net frames have been made and used successfully by many hunters of big fish. They have one major disadvantage in that they do not fold away and are thus rather bulky. However, they are very light in weight, very strong, and easy to make. The first problem is to obtain a lightweight spring rim from a cyclist friend or accessory shop; one that is slightly buckled will do perfectly well. Saw this across, preferably at one of the joins, then push the two ends together so that they overlap by about 2 in. and tape them together. Finally, drill a hole through both overlapping parts so that a $\frac{3}{8}$ in. bolt can be pushed through from the inside of the circle. To take the landing net handle about an inch of bolt needs to be projecting.

TRIANGULAR

There is such a variety of these available commercially, and made in amateur fashion by anglers, that it is difficult to know which type of construction to recommend. Although we do not rate any of them as highly as a round frame, we have made and experimented with a number of different designs. Of these, the type illustrated in Photo. 45 is one of the best we have used. The design is simple and easy to make.

The arms are straight ash for preference, but other good straight-grained woods can be used. At the handle end of the frame the cross-section of the arms should be square and they should be bolted or screwed to the open-V-shaped flats, the angles of these flats (aluminium or black mild steel) being chosen to suit the preferred spread of the landing net arms. The two small projections on one flat fit into drilled holes in the other, thus avoiding any twist when the two flats are pulled up together.

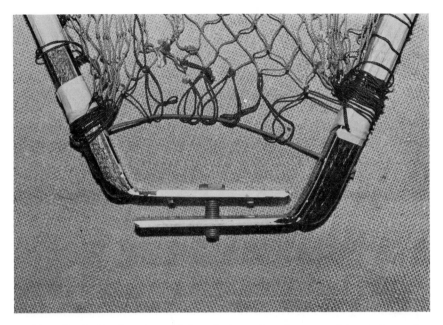

45 Detail of duralumin and beech junction for attaching triangular landing net to handle: open V-shaped duralumin plates set into beech arms also visible.

If mild steel is used in the construction these projections can be welded on; in the case of aluminium (or similarly strengthened metal alloys) it is better to drill holes and fit them with tight bolts of short projection.

LANDING NET HANDLES

There are two distinct types of landing net handle – long, and short! The long handle is usually favoured by the coarse fisherman and, more recently, the reservoir fly fisherman. It also finds favour with those who wade, when its duties double as a wading staff, something very necessary where uneven river beds and slippery rocks must be clambered over.

It is possible to purchase a threaded ferrule in various sizes which will wedge-fit on to the handle and into which the net may be screwed (Photo. 45). All that remains is to find a suitable length of tubular material (4 ft is the average) that will be strong enough to support the net and, in certain cases, the weight of the angler. The most common material is a length of cane, which can be trimmed at top and bottom close to a node, and filed to allow the passage of the net ferrule. Once rigged, and with the addition of a rubber button at the bottom end (à la walking stick) the tool is complete. An annual coat of varnish is a must – but with all the care in the world, the cane will ultimately crack, and allow water to enter and rot its hollow interior.

Far better and naturally more expensive, is a length of glass fibre. Plug each end with a cork pushed just down inside the bore before offering up the ferrule and end button, and the handle will remain watertight. Water cannot rot glass fibre – but it will weight it so that should the handle be dropped into the water it will sink. We definitely prefer a floating handle; hence our insistence on the plug and the end button.

There is a lot to be said for a fixed net, something in the fashion of a prawn-fisherman's large scoop net, or a stag net, especially where the angler lives close to the water he will fish. For this,

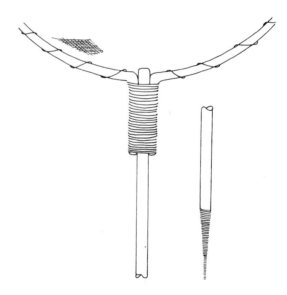

Fig. **E** Fixed landing net construction with stout pole bound to robust rim by copper wire, and sharpened base of pole, also bound with copper wire.

the best handle is that used for a broom, to which the rim of the net, hollow tubular alloy, can be fitted with the mesh before both ends are whipped on the pole by means of copper wire. The beauty of a thick wooden handle is that the end can be shaped, and the point wrapped with copper or other suitable metal, making a useful aid where really slippery ground has to be crossed. Fig. **E** shows construction details.

Short landing net handles, favoured by the game fisherman, can be made from cane or glass fibre, fitted with a ferrule or the frame rim bound directly to the body, and provided with a grip of some sort at the handle (lower) end. Strip leather (used for the rod handle) and heavy cord can be bound and glued into place, or a slightly under-sized rubber hand-grip eased on the end with a little glue, and left to dry.

Carrying a short-handled net is difficult. Left swinging off a loop on the jacket it tends to twist between one's legs, causing accidents! Dangled off a length of elastic, as we know from bitter experience, it can cause some nasty incidents when the net catches on bankside herbage and then suddenly flies free. We sling ours across our back, using a dog lead. The handle end of the lead is whipped at the hand end of the handle, and the net is then slung across the back with the mesh downwards.

The leash is carried over the shoulder and across the front of the body where the clip can be latched to the rim of the net itself. When required the clip is released, the net drops down and it can be grabbed and swung into position with the minimum of fuss. If this presents a problem to more spherical anglers, the leash can be abandoned and the release clip whipped to a suitable length of nylon cord.

DYEING LINES

There can be little doubt that many lines, particularly monofils, are too shiny and too brightly coloured, and that most serious anglers look for dull, dark, supple yet hard lines. Dullness is something which comes to most lines after a few hours' use, and the colour can be simply and quickly changed by dyeing. We used to worry about the effect of hot dye upon the line strength, but experience has established that it has no effect as far as practical angling is concerned. Plaited lines take colour more easily than monofil partly because the colour is held in the folds between strands, but even a lightly-dyed monofil is better than a shiny white or blue one.

We use Dylon dyes, and usually make them up to 2–3 times the recommended dyeing strength, at least when colouring monofil – the dark browns and blacks being preferred. If you have an old-fashioned tackle winder and a large plastic bucket then you have the perfect equipment. Boil the water, add the dye, and stir it up well. Allow it to go off the boil and drop in the winder. It can be left in for hours, occasionally warming up the dye, depending upon how dark you prefer the colour to be and on the particular batch of line, for they all vary.

It is possible to drop in the line spool as bought, but the disadvantages are that spools are usually plastic and they may burst (being hot and under pressure they usually do) and that the line deep on the spool takes the dye less well. Nevertheless, this is how we do it nowadays and it is effective enough. Care must be taken when winding off the line on to the reel to avoid tangles resulting from the burst plastic spool. Plaited nylons and terylene take on a lovely hue, with little effort. There are anglers who claim that a 'transparent' line is best in water but we are unconvinced and continue to favour a drab, dark line which we feel is far more natural.

SNAP TACKLES (LIVE & DEADBAIT RIGS)

Naturally, the variety of tackle under this heading varies almost as much as the individual, but the rig described here is one which has caught literally hundreds of double-figure pike, over fifty twenty-pounders, on both live and deadbait, and in every conceivable sense can be classed as first-rate home-made equipment. In our opinion this snap tackle is far superior to any commercial brand we have yet seen.

Needed for making the snap tackle are various sizes of treble hooks, mostly sizes 6 and 8, with an eye at the top of the shank as opposed to a tapered shank eyeless hook; some Ryder treble hooks in the same sizes; some small swivels and a reel of cabled wire such as Tidemaster, Alasticum, or similar type. The last is almost the most important item. Were it possible to obtain wire of 12–14 lb b.s. then that is what we would use, but in fact 20 lb b.s. is about the thinnest on the market at present. It is certainly thinner than monofil of the same breaking strain and much thinner than the wire on most shop-bought tackles, so it is quite satisfactory. The wire should be dark and supple yet soft enough to enable two short pieces to be overlapped and twisted together with the fingers without resorting to pliers. Alasticum is good in this respect but is a fraction too loosely cabled so that it opens up along its length with not much excuse. Tidemaster is almost but not quite too strong to be twisted with the fingers, and we rate it best of the current wires.

The first step is to cut an 18 in. length of wire, and to pass one end through the eye of a treble hook, laying it back along itself for about 1 in. The wire can be passed twice through the eye if this gives the angler extra confidence. Next, twist the two por-

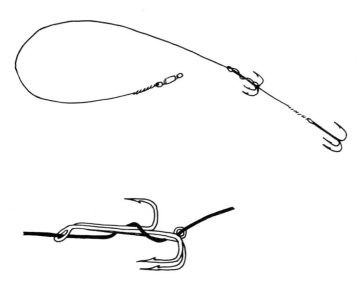

Fig. F The traditional Jardine snap tackle for piking, rated by the authors as the best bait rig of all. Constructed of cabled wire (e.g. Alasticum, Tidemaster etc.), swivel, fixed lower treble, and *sliding* Ryder Hook (also shown enlarged).

tions together so that you have less than an inch of twist above the hook and along the wire. Then add a Ryder hook of the same size (hooked end first) to the wire trace, wrapping the latter once or twice round the shank (depending upon how stiffly it slides) and finally out through the Ryder hook eye at the other end of the shank. When moving such a hook up and down the trace do it slowly and carefully by a 'passing the loops' system rather than wrenching it along quickly; the latter results in a broad spiral twist to the whole trace. Finally, attach the swivel at the top end by exactly the same method as that used on the eye of the first treble hook. The length of the trace should be around 15 in. and the twisted portions can be strengthened with glue. However, if they have been twisted together properly they will not pull apart no matter how large the pike or how long the fight.

For pike fishing, larger hooks than sizes 6 and 8 are unnecessary except on plugs and spoons, and when wobbling deadbaits on a one treble system. The trace for the latter is exactly the same as the above, except that the Ryder hook is omitted. Multihook rigs we have no time for nowadays since we use baits in the 1–7 oz range rather than large baits, but should multihook rigs, 'instant strike rigs', single hook rigs, etc., be required, they can be built on exactly the same principles and with just the same materials as above.

LIVE AND DEADBAIT RIGS (alternative schemes)

These items are simple to make, and an evening's work can supply enough terminal tackle to keep the angler going over a whole season. They all feature a treble or series of treble hooks fastened to a length of Alasticum cable, and a swivel at the terminal end which will, in turn, be fastened to the line.

DEADBAIT RIGS

Start by passing the end of a 9 in. length of cabled Alasticum trace through the eye of a treble hook so that an inch or so of loose end is left. This in turn is then bound round the long trace part in a series of tight twists, close to the eye of the treble, until most of the short end is used up. Aim to get the turns as close together as possible, a good method being to fasten one end of the trace in a vice, threading the other end of it through the treble's eye, and then twisting the short end into place, holding the treble in the fingers of the left hand and stretching the trace wire as tightly as possible. The right hand with the short end will be able to produce very small, tight turns that will be unlikely to unravel when strain is applied. Snip off the trace end that cannot be turned in, rub a little Araldite glue over the join, and the job is done.

Additional hooks can be knotted on the trace very easily. Position the treble where it is required with the shank lying flush against the wire trace. Pass the loose end through the eye of the treble, double it back behind the bend of one of the three hooks, then bind it tightly round and up the shank of the hook over the trace some five or six times. Next, pass the end through the eye once more taking care not to cause a kink, and the rig is complete.

If it is not intended to thread the trace through a deadbait by means of a baiting needle then a swivel, or snap-fastening swivel, can be bound on the free end in the same way that the end treble was mounted; but do take care with the Araldite sealing – any which gets on the swivel will bind it and prevent it working. If it *is* intended as a threaded trace, then use a very small swivel.

A few deadbait mounts consist of two trebles mounted on the trace itself which will fasten along the bait's body in the accepted way, and a large single hook that is passed through the lips or head of the bait to prevent it from breaking away during a long cast. When preparing this type of rig, mount the two fixed trebles, but only pass the trace once through the eye of the single hook. When the bait is offered into position and the single hook is pushed into place, the free end of the trace can be threaded once more through the eye, locking it tightly.

LIVEBAIT RIGS

The accepted snap tackle for livebaiting purchased from a tackle shop will have the usual treble mounted at the end of the trace, with a second mounted on the middle of the trace, and which possesses a small eye soldered just above the bend of the hooks. The trace passes through this eye, is wound several times round the shank, and then passes through the normal eye, making an adjustable treble that can be slid up or down the trace to suit the size of bait employed. Sliding this treble about tends to stretch and distort the wire, and some anglers consider it better to have a collection of fixed mounts with a varying distance between the first and second treble, allowing one to be selected that will fit the size of livebait that is used. In other words, the deadbait rig already described will serve equally well for the livebait mount.

By far the biggest curse of live and deadbait mounts is storing and carrying them ready for use. In the section on tackle boxes on page 118, and immediately below, we discuss and illustrate methods of trouble-free carrying, and we recommend you to look at these for suitable ideas.

SNAP TACKLE HOLDER

These hold not only snap tackles but also wire traces and anything else that you might think is at risk of getting kinked. When Barrie made his original version, which evolved from a genuine Yule log used by Ray Webb, he used a baby's dried milk tin, but today it is far better to get hold of a plastic container. Rian Tingay uses the outside container from a large Thermos flask. Select your container first, before attempting to design its contents.

Assuming you have obtained a cylindrical container, prepare a piece of balsa, circular in cross section, with a diameter about 2 in. less than the container's inside diameter. The length of balsa log should be about 1 in. less than the length of the container. Next you need a couple of circular end boards (plywood or hardboard), each with a diameter which gives a clearance of about a couple of millimetres when inside the container. These should be glued and screwed to the ends of the balsa log. The swivels of your snap tackles can now be secured to the wall of the balsa with round-topped mapping pins. The 1 in. clearance in the

46 Snap tackle holder of balsa wood.

47 Snap tackle holder of polystyrene block which fits into Tupperware box.

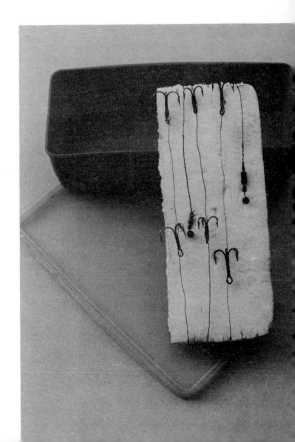

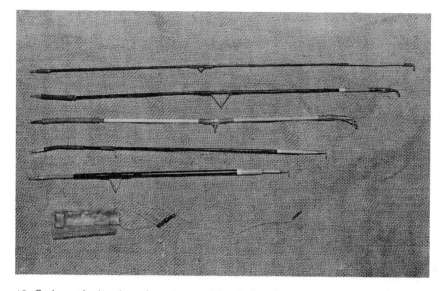

48 Quiver tip (top), swing tips and leaded swim feeder; all are very easy to make. The length and weight of all materials can be varied to suit different conditions.

length of balsa within the container allows for a small plastic handle to be added for easy withdrawal.

Barrie has been using a holder of this kind for well over ten years and, unlike its owner, it shows no sign of deterioration.

FISHING BOXES

Some anglers delight in humping fishing tackle around and are never happier than when they are festooned with bags, boxes and a trolley with wheels that groan, buckle and squeak under excessive weight. At the other end of the scale is the man who sticks two or three flies in the lapel of his jacket, stuffs a spare cast in his pocket, and ambles off along the river bank confident that he can cope with any emergency.

Possibly Freud would have had interesting comments to make on both approaches; but on reflection it would be unfair to draw comparisons in human nature. We would clear our yard-arm by

49 Terry clips – an ideal way of storing rods in the back of a wardrobe.

stating that we try to place ourselves somewhere between the supremely confident and extremely worried approach.

Tackle must be carried, and where it is carried it should be protected from damage both during the journey and along the bank where the angler fishes. It must also be protected from wet and dirt – which by and large means the effects of the weather. All of which points to a box-type container of some sort (or a rucksack) and there are dozens of various sizes and shapes available in tackle shops, constructed from nearly as many types of material. The unfortunate thing is that many boxes are purchased at the shop without any attempt being made to relate them to the assorted pieces of tackle that will eventually be carried in them.

What are the ideals that should govern the choice of a tackle box? Well, as we have already noted, it must be made from strong material. Of course, one does not normally throw tackle around on the banks, but it *is* possible to sit or fall on a fishing bag or jacket, and a box therein that immediately collapses is worthless. But it must also be light (in weight) and be fitted out inside so that everything will fit comfortably without bulging the lid, otherwise the box cannot shut – and it will certainly not be watertight.

Size is all-important. Too big a box will allow the items inside to bounce around, frightening the fish and infuriating fellow-anglers. In addition, the contents will certainly form an unholy jumble and tangle, and while your consequent flow of invective might excite envy and admiration, your angling prowess will not be improved. Too small a box may be useful at first, but it is a safe assumption that it will ultimately finish up inside a bigger one – the box-within-a-box syndrome that leads to unnecessary weight and a schizophrenic personality. Finally, the fastenings, of whatever type, must be simple and easy enough to be opened with cold, wet fingers, but positive enough to ensure that they do not open of their own accord – a pre-requisite for disaster.

All of which brings us to the crunch, which is whether it is better to purchase new, purpose-designed boxes; to adapt something already in our possession or purchased from the shop; or finally, to design and tailor-make a box for the items that have to be carried – or which we consider essential for our needs. Well, new boxes are very nice, but with today's high cost of plastic, the larger sizes (which include fitted-out boxes for spinners, plugs and match fishing tackle, etc.) are a bit heavy on the pocket. More especially when the tackle collection grows, and either a bigger model or duplicate of the original box has to be purchased.

These large boxes are rarely carried by the angler along the bank whilst fishing. Mostly they are stock boxes left at home or in the holiday accommodation, and used as a reservoir from which missing items can be replaced. We have found that tool boxes fitted out with trays, and sold in umpteen large stores and car-spare shops to be as practical as the generally more expensive tackle shop item. They are capable of being sub-divided by sheet plastic, glued into position, until a very passable box has been fitted to suit the individual's requirements. In fact, by checking against today's prices at discount shops, it is possible to buy two of these tool boxes for the price of one near-identical container that has been custom built by the tackle manufacturer – and which will not necessarily accommodate your particular requirements.

Some custom built boxes available from tackle shops are excellent value for money, and we admire those with a clear transparent lid, which enables the item required to be immediately seen, a big time-saver on the bank. But, of course, one must adapt one's tackle to fit into the pre-determined shapes – sometimes no easy matter. It is possible to remove partition walls by breaking them out with a pair of square-nosed pliers, but this is always a risky job that can go sour, and cause a fracture of an outer wall. Partitions that are too big and in which tackle rattles around can be 'deadened' by cutting and glueing thin foam plastic or, better still, Ethafoam, to the bottom.

Next to consider are the odd boxes that can be found around the house, especially tobacco and cigarette tins, small biscuit tins, etc. Some of these can be fitted out, although fitting the partitions can be a problem. Ken uses 2 oz tobacco tins for holding small spinners, and fits them out in a special way. Simply loading an assortment of lures loosely into the box –

50 A tobacco-tin spinning box. The polystyrene bar into which hooks are pushed has been coloured for ease of identification.

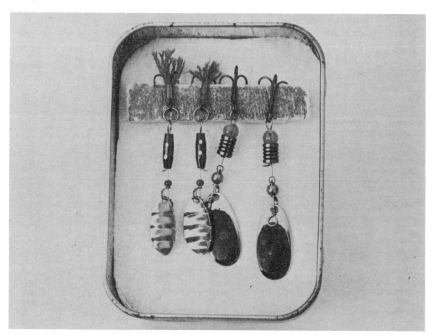

even if it is padded with foam of some sort at the top and bottom
– leads to a mass of jumbled hooks and bodies that causes chip-
ping and scratching to both angler and lures. The only answer
when carrying spinners is to secure them in place against the
box – quite a simple matter. Once the box has been padded, find a
piece of polystyrene foam from an old packing case, or easier
perhaps, the decorators' coving that is sold to fit around the
edge of ceilings and walls. Cut a piece that is long enough to
fit across the width of the box and approximately $\frac{1}{4}$ in. thick.
Glue this an inch inside one end of the tin and leave it to dry.
Now spinners can be hooked on to the strip by the end treble
and laid flat. Once the lid is on, the box can be stored on end in a
pocket or partition pocket of the tackle bag, where the spinners
will hang vertically, unable to bunch or tangle. Photo. 50 shows
the idea. To ensure that the box is stored with the hooks uppermost, we paint the outside of that end of the tin red.

In the household category one must include the various
Tuppaware type boxes that are on the market, and these form
excellent protective containers for larger items of tackle. We
say larger items advisedly. The lid to these airtight boxes are, of
necessity, a tight fit and often considerable force from the
fingertips is needed to open them. Imagine the box loaded with
small items, and the possible result when that extra bit of pressure is applied – it opens with a bang, and away goes the contents all over the bank. We know; we have done it. Floats, swim
feeders, spare disgorgers (one is best fastened to the lapel of a
jacket whilst fishing), packets containing ready-tied hooks –
these are all fine, but split shot, loose hooks, etc. are best kept
separately outside this type of receptacle.

We grew tired of adapting boxes and for some years we have
been manufacturing our own to suit our own particular requirements. By doing this we make sure that the tackle fits the boxes,
and more important that the box fits into a pocket or partition
of the shoulder bag or rucksack that is carried. There is dis-
agreement between us as to choice of materials. Ken favours
wood, whilst Barrie uses plastic – but both are light, strong and
easy to make up. Here are construction details for two types of
box that can be modified in many ways to suit practically everything that has to be carried.

WOODEN BOXES

Photo. 51 shows an exploded view of all the odd parts required for a fly box. The top and bottom is cut from an offcut of Formica – they cost pence, depending on their size, from a D.I.Y. shop, and several boxes can be made from the one piece. The beauty of this material is that it is light, easy to clean and the variety of colours and patterns enables immediate identification of each box; as an example, red for dry flies, green for wet, etc. As a further aid, Ken uses white for one side of all his boxes, and a colour for the other. The white side makes an ideal background against which one can change a fly, tie a knot, etc. even in the poorest visibility. An excellent idea which would certainly have occurred to Barrie at some time during the next decade.

The top and bottom of the illustrated box are 6×4 in., which will fit into most pockets with ease. The sides are cut from $\frac{1}{2} \times \frac{1}{4}$ in. planed battens, four pieces 6 in. long, four pieces $3\frac{1}{2}$ in. long. These are then glued in along the edges of both top and

51 Component parts for a fly-box. Formica top and bottom; battens; clasp and hinges.

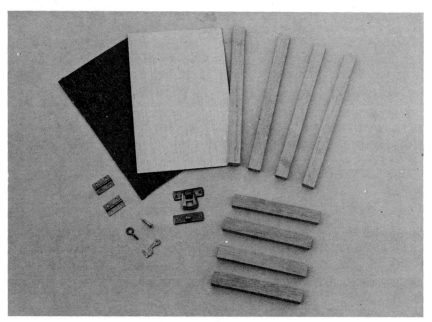

bottom pieces, thus forming two trays. Use one of the strong, instant-binding glues on the market, taking care to spread the glue thinly but evenly – mistakes with these glues are nearly always impossible to rectify.

Small $\frac{1}{4}$ in. brass hinges can now be secured on one side of both top and bottom, or let into the edges as shown in Photo. 52 A small brass hook and eye, or snap clasp, can be mounted on the opposite side from the hinges, and the assembly is complete. Small gaps (yes, they do occur) where the side pieces butt against each other can be filled with plastic wood, and the sides then stained and varnished with a good copal varnish. Two sheets of Ethafoam can be cut to fit the interior, secured in place with a little glue, and the job is done.

Variations? Well, anything you fancy. Two strips of polystyrene or cork, mounted in the same manner as described for the tobacco tin box, and the whole thing can be used for spinning lures. Increase the sizes – using deeper battens for the sides – for

52 The finished fly-box.

bigger baits. Increase the length, glue strips of plastic foam at intervals across the width of the box, cut slots into these, and a whole series of floats can be held firmly in place. Compare the cost of producing these boxes with the shop-bought item, and you will quickly find that you are showing a handsome profit.

PLASTIC BOXES

We have always been advocates of the use of natural materials, but where boxes are concerned plastic has the same relationship to wood as it does in rod making. Our use of plastic in box making was encouraged by David Holden, practical angler extraordinary, who discovered that Slater's plasticard in various thicknesses could be easily cut and glued.

All that is needed is a ruler and a Stanley knife. Hinges and catches are merely added in the manner already described. Photo. 54 shows a finished box with the lid held in the position it will be when hinged. Most D.I.Y. shops sell a special glue for

53 Basic materials for plastic box construction as described in text.

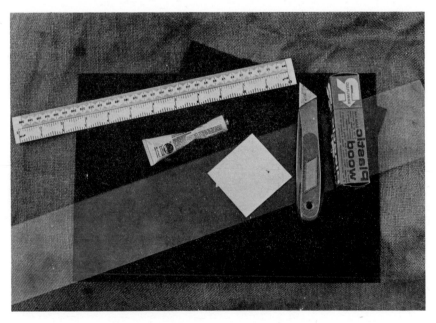

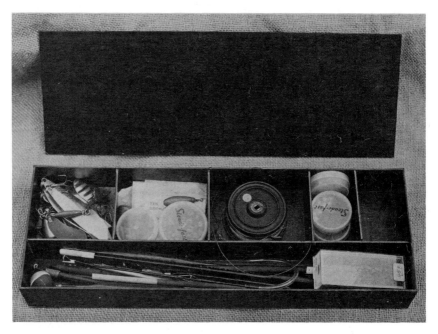

54 The completed plastic box.

plasticard and it is certainly best to use this, although the one
shown was glued with Durafix – an adhesive which also has the
unfortunate effect, if used in any quantity other than a thin
film, of dissolving the plastic!

Cut out the base of the box from a sheet of plasticard. Do this
by scoring along the edge of a steel ruler, using a Stanley knife.
It is not necessary to cut deeper than 1 mm into the card, after
which it snaps easily and cleanly. For larger boxes than shown,
use a thicker card for the base than the walls, but as a general
rule it will be found that 1·5 mm card is about right. The sides
are cut in exactly the same way and glueing is achieved by
smearing one edge thinly with glue and then simply holding it
in the required position. After about a minute or so a 'soft' bond
is obtained and you can proceed with the next side. Care should
be taken to make the partitions a good fit, neither loose nor
unduly tight, so that the glue does its work well.

The most easily obtained plasticard sheets are 230 × 330 mm
and cost less than £1 each. A box of the kind illustrated can be
made in under an hour for less than one quarter the usual price.

SPECIAL BOXES

Of all the angling items that have to be carried, live and deadbait mounts for pike fishing are probably the most difficult to stow away effectively. Stored loosely they tangle; stored in separate plastic packets they still manage to tangle when the hooks stick through the sides of the packet. This problem we have both solved by constructing a special box that enables each rig to be individually stretched and mounted on a block, where it can be selected, released and used without the risk of tangling.

Ken uses an oblong Tupperware box, into which fits a piece of stiff polystyrene foam (see Photo. 47). The foam is a good inch thinner than the depth of the box, and the various live and dead-bait rigs are mounted on this by pushing the end hook into the foam itself, winding the trace around the length of the block, and finally securing it with a map pin through the eye of the swivel. Our photo shows the idea – and of course, the map pins can be colour coded, different colours being used to denote dead or livebait rigs, hook sizes, etc.

Barrie designed the log box some years ago, and this has become quite famous (see Photo. 46).

ROD RESTS

If someone, in fifty years time, prepares an historical précis of rod rests we feel sure it will not only fill several tomes, but boggle the mind with the variety exhibited. The match angling world is largely responsible for the modern proliferation of rod rests, and whilst the same root cause has enhanced the possibilities of float fishing we remain uncertain whether it has done much for resting rods. The rod rests about to be described we rate as second to none for most fishing, excluding match fishing, and yet a very similar commercial make was recently described as useless by a leading match fisherman. The match angler needs somewhere soft on to which he can quickly place, or even drop his rod: for him, the best solution is a strung rubber between arms about a foot apart, or a rubber-covered wire in the same position. Countless numbers are available commercially – usually offered at exorbitant prices.

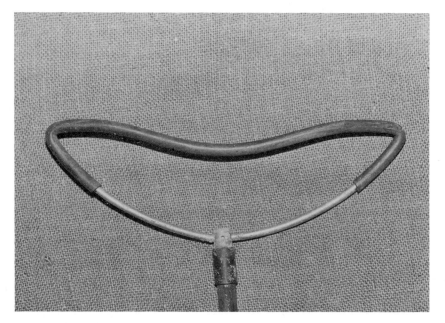

55 Matchman's simple rod rest: the rubber tube is stretched between aluminium arms which are passed through the head of an alloy bolt.

For the rest of us, we need something that will hold the rod in anything but a force nine gale, and yet let the line run out unhindered in pike, eel and carp fishing. There is scope for enormous improvement in the rod rest heads supplied by commercial enterprises. For the most part they are much too wide: most rods have a diameter of less than 1½ in. and the spread of the rest needs to be that *at a maximum*. This makes it both lighter, and less bulky in the holdall. The one illustrated among the batch in Photo. 56 is ideal, and is simply made by bending a coat-hanger wire into the required shape with pliers, and then Araldite it into the top of a piece of tank aerial or similar lightweight tube. The bottom of the rod rest is shown to its right: a sharpened piece of aluminium tap fitted into the tube. The whole rest can then be painted dark green or black. The only commercial efforts which come close are the plastic green ones which screw into a standard bankstick thread. These have the drawback of being weak, and they snap at the slightest provocation. Nevertheless, it should not be beyond the imagination of

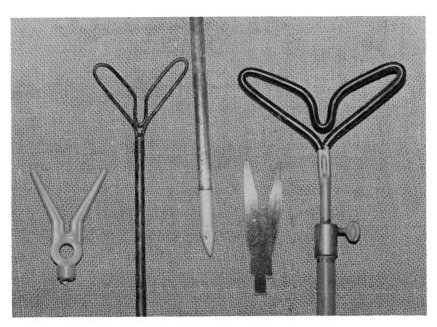

56 Home-made rod rest, second and third from left, compared with commercial products at left and right. The prototype for a much simpler rest is shown second from right.

commerce to come up with a screw-in head the width of which is even less than the one described.

An improvement on our own suggestion, simple and effective though that is, would be to have the small wire head glued or welded to a standard bolt (preferably small and light) which could then be screwed into a standard duralumin bankstick. Rod rest heads could then be carried in the basket or rucksack, and the standard banksticks could also be used for keepnets, weed cutting heads, or for electric bite indicators.

RUBBY DUBBY

These are most commonly used in sea fishing, often being no more than a mesh bag tied to the anchor rope just above the anchor itself. They are little used in freshwater fishing, but we have used them effectively from boats in exactly the same way as they are used by sea anglers, and from the shore by throwing out a wire roll in which fish offal is wrapped (the whole being attached to a rope, naturally!). This latter method ensures that the attractor is not eaten by the eels, pike, etc. and can be retrieved easily at intervals. A second method now under experiment is to freeze a ball of minced fish around a nut or weight that is sufficient to sink it. Since this is a non-retrievable object lead weights should *not* be used. As the ball thaws a slow trickle of juices and aroma is released into the water. Delicious! – at least, the fish think so.

WEED AND REED CUTTER

For this highly efficient piece of equipment (which cuts rather than drags weeds out by the roots) we use a 15 in. length of conduit tubing with an external diameter of $\frac{3}{4}$ in. Into this is inserted an 18 in. blade of mild black steel having a thickness of $\frac{1}{8}$ in. and a width of nearly 2 in. Cut a slot in one end of the

57 The weed cutter, as described.

conduit tubing fractionally over $\frac{1}{8}$ in. wide to accept the blade, which can then be lightly welded in position. Use a coarse bastard file to put a cutting edge on the conduit tubing side of the blade: it does not have to be razor sharp, and can be sharpened up again in minutes with the same file. The loose ring fitted at the other end of the conduit tube is simply a point of attachment for the rope.

This cutter is quite big and needs a powerful throw, but it is relatively easy to scale down. For example, the blade itself could be 2 in. shorter at either end, and $\frac{1}{2}$ in. narrower, whilst still being very effective. Very soft weeds are not, of course, easily cut by any device, but we guarantee that this cutter will remove reeds as easily as it does pond weed (potamogeton).

WEED DRAG

As with the round landing net frame and the cutter, mild black steel is used for this. The illustration is largely self-explanatory.

58 The weed drag, as described.

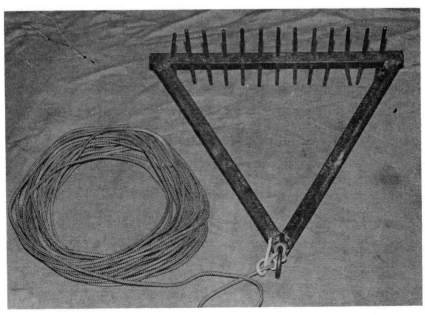

Three pieces of steel, $18 \times 1 \times \frac{3}{16}$ in. are welded to form a triangle. One side is drilled with holes at $1\frac{1}{4}$ in. intervals of such diameter to take 6 in. rods of $\frac{1}{4}$ in. diameter. These are welded so that 3 in. projects on either side. A loop of steel is added for rope attachment.

This is a heavy drag, weighing 4 lbs, which a reasonably strong angler can throw for perhaps fifteen yards: ideal for a tench fishing swim. But it can be made lighter by making it T-shaped, though it would be unwise to cut down on the weight of metal. It is important that the pulling end of the drag, whether T-shaped or two sides of a triangle, should be welded to the tooth-holding portion and should not be, as some amateur jobs are, a matter of attaching a rope only to the tooth-holding portion. The latter make poor drags because the head of the drag rotates as soon as it carries a heavy load of weed, with the result that at least half the effectiveness is lost.

CAR ROD RACKS

Little time will be spent on this item, important though it is, for commercial racks for fitting *outside* the car are both efficient and reasonably priced. Someone better at do-it-yourself than your authors could copy a patented model quite easily, but as we said earlier, copying manufactured goods is not the aim of this enterprise.

However, internal rod racks to hold rods in their bags is something rarely seen but of great value and efficiency. We heard of this many years ago, but first saw it used by Pete and Janet Jackson, of the Tenchfishers' Club, in their fishing van. The system cannot easily be used in cars, but in vans and estate waggons it can work well. First you need a number of polythene drain pipes of various diameters. These should be cut to the appropriate length and fitted like a set of horizontal organ pipes to the inside of the van roof. The openings should be at the back, so that when the rear doors are opened rods etc. can quite easily be pulled out. Such a system is excellent for preserving rods from the dangers of big feet, heavy boxes and so on, and eliminates the need for that enormous holdall kicking around the back of the vehicle. The tricky part of the operation is attaching the pipes to the roof of the van, and the method depends on the nature of the van itself. In some vans it is possible to spring a couple of holding bars across the roof and below the tubes: in this case you need foam above the racks to help quieten any rattles. We have also heard that attachment can be made with strips of Velcro, but have not seen this in use and have no experience of it. Probably the easiest way is to drill holes in the roof, and equally probably no-one wants to do this. In general, some kind of frame is needed to span the roof below the tubes, and it occurs to us that some use might be made of sheets of corrugated plastic roofing.

LINE DISPENSERS

A great many anglers today, an increasing number, use bulk spools from which to fill their reels with reel line. This is not only much cheaper but enables you to fill any reel spool to the brim without going through the rigmarole of first putting the line on

59 Line dispenser for bulk spools.

the reel followed by backing, and then reversing the whole process. Naturally, you need several bulk spools: ours are of 15 lb b.s.; 11/12 lb b.s.; 6 lb b.s.; 5 lb b.s. and 4 lb b.s. Finer lines we buy on the ordinary small spools. A good way of both storing and dispensing such spools is to take a 2 ft plank of wood of about 6 in. × ½ in. width and thickness and at intervals along it glue or screw 4 in. lengths of dowel rod in a vertical position. The bulk spools are simply slotted on to them. The dowel rods need to be of various diameters from broom handle down to, perhaps, pencil thickness, since the hole through the middle of a bulk spool is non-standard. Five or six bulk spools can then be placed in a line, put on a cool shelf, and covered over with a dark cloth to keep out all light. It is a simple matter to load a reel with line: simply tie on and reel on slowly and carefully. The dowel rods should not be shorter than 4–6 in., otherwise too much wobble and twist ensues during the process. Tension can be quickly adjusted by draping a cloth on the line, trapping it loosely to the table or the floor about a yard in front of the reel.

ANCHORS

It is possible to buy proper anchors, but not only are they expensive (though admittedly efficient) but they seem to belong to the realms of boating people rather than anglers. We use a boat for fishing, nothing else, and the anchors consist of various sized concrete blocks with rings in the top. They are easily made by filling plastic buckets (or a hole in the ground lined with polythene) with concrete and firmly anchoring a large ring-headed screw in the top, or a ¼ in. diameter length of black mild steel bent into a loop. It is better to attach it to some wire netting and to sink this into the concrete as well, for otherwise the ring eventually pulls out. We have seen cans filled with concrete, with the can handle used for the rope attachment, but these have a short life and the tin becomes dangerous as it rusts. Since it is just as easy to make more permanent concrete blocks there seems little point in using tin cans.

One worthwhile tip: on a boat fishing expedition always take your own anchors with you. In our experience, boat-yard anchors come in two categories: non-existent and inadequate.

60 Simple mud anchors.

SOFT SEATS

One of the luxuries of modern angling results from foam being available in offcuts in various shapes, sizes and composition. They can be cut to shape for almost any basket or bag and can be rolled up quite tightly when they soften – as they do after a few outings. Less happily, tight rolling shortens the life of the foam. It is a good idea to put the foam in a plastic bag such as a dustbin bag. Do *not* seal the bag since although this results in a more pneumatic seat, it is also more difficult to store.

For boat fishing, where bulk during loading can be important, an inflatable inner tube is better than foam. Small inner tubes are best, such as those used for trailer wheels. They make comfortable seats and in an emergency they add to the buoyancy of the individual's life-jacket following a capsize.

THOLE PINS

Messing about in boats can be a dangerous business and we do not propose to deal with boat maintenance: it is a subject best left to boat experts and any would-be D.I.Y. angler would be advised to consult such experts before making any *major* changes to his craft. Normal maintenance, such as painting, is not directly relevant to fishing (except that we paint the hull a dark hue) and it would be superfluous to deal with such things here. But small alterations to boats are easily undertaken by the keen angler. Elsewhere we have mentioned anchors and boat rod rests, and thole pins are something else that few boats outside Eire possess.

Most boats have rowlocks, and whilst these are perfect for skilful rowing when rowing is the objective, for anglers they are next to useless and must be a contributory factor to at least some dangerous situations in which anglers find themselves. Oars jump out of rowlocks, and slide out of them, at the slightest inattention on the part of the angler. Thole pins (Fig. **G**) hold an oar *locked* if you let go of it, and in trolling that is something you need to do quickly without the distraction of losing an oar.

The diagram is self-explanatory, and no dimensions are given because these depend upon the dimensions of the gunwhale

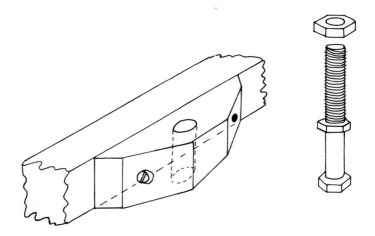

Fig. **G** Basic thole pin construction. Dimensions are chosen to fit gunwhale (on left). The same structure is attached to one side of each oar.

board to which they are attached by copper screws or brass bolts. The pin itself, coming through from beneath, has a diameter of perhaps $\frac{3}{4}$ in. and projects about 6 in. The best ones have a thread on the top to which a nut can be screwed so that there is no chance at all of the oar jumping off the pin. Ideally, the pin should be tight-fitting in its mount, by use of glue and nut where it comes out of the wooden block, but loose-fitting in the oar block.

The oar block is made in exactly the same fashion as the pin block, except that it has no pin through the hole, which latter should have a diameter of about an inch for the example quoted above. Again, the size of the oar block is governed by the size of the oar, and a concave base to it may be necessary to ensure a flush fit to the oar prior to screwing.

The combination of thole pin and oar should never be so placed that the oar cannot be shipped, or largely shipped, upon landing. So fix everything in position temporarily before finally deciding on the best place. In most boats there is little trouble.

BIAFRAN HORSES

The description of this piece of equipment results from the scathing comment by a fellow-angler that these rests resemble starving horses, and since Biafra was in the news at the time such rod rests became popular, the name stuck with them.

Once again you need a welding friend; 2–3 ft of $\frac{1}{4}$ in. mild black steel, and a G-clamp – preferably one with a broadly-based grip. G-clamps are expensive, but we feel that the efficiency of this form of boat rod rest justifies its purchase. Photos. 61 and 62 give a clearer impression of the make-up than any written description, but it is necessary to say that the angle of the supporting wire may need to be adjusted after the piece of equipment has been clamped on the gunwhale. The covering of plastic adhesive tape, by the way, is not for decorative purposes: it minimises wear on the rods.

The butt of the rod is placed in the downward facing bend of the hook, and the more forward part is dropped into the V. It is an advantage to have the reel *beyond* the rest, which works well

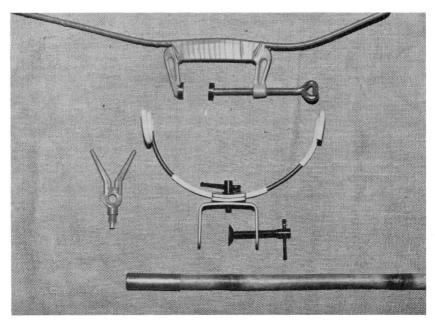

61 Biafran horses (see text); simple landing net handle at bottom; repaired commercial rod rest top (cf. Photo. 56) to left.

62 Russian boat rod rest in position on gunwhale.

with long-handled specimen hunting rods, but the total length of the rest cannot be too short otherwise it does not have the strength of leverage to hold the rod without a lot of sag.

Although these rests have been in use in this country, at least commonly, for a decade, they have been made in the Soviet Union for many years, but only for small rods including jigging equipment. The one shown in Photo. 62 will not hold a heavy British rod because the clamp is too weak.

TENCH FISHING SCREEN

A most neglected item of tackle this, yet easy to make, easy to carry and seriously affecting the quality of any short range fishing. We call it a tench fishing screen, but that is only because

Fig. **H** Camouflaged screen shown attached to rod rests by draw-strings.

we first came across it in that context being used by an old friend, Eric Hodson. Eric, incidentally, was responsible for passing on quite a few of the ideas in this book, including the rod rests described earlier. Quite simply, this item is a screen which you position in front of you whilst fishing at close range. Stretched between two long duralumin banksticks, is a piece of material 3 ft high and 4 ft long. In practice, the length can be shortened by rolling up the material on one of the rests, and the height can be changed by sliding the material down both rests. Ideally, about 2 ft is the best height, for it means that you can sit behind it on quite a large chair or basket and yet be totally out of sight of the fish.

The material used can be nylon lace curtain material (it is not necessary to buy flower-patterned pieces!) dyed with Dylon dyes as described on page 112. There are also green plastic perforated materials available which need no dyeing, and which seem to stay cleaner than more conventional curtain material. Both can be camouflage-dyed, but we do not bother with such refinements: ours are in plain dark green. The rests themselves can be threaded in and out along the short edges of the plastic material, but it is necessary to stretch the lace curtaining along the rests so that it is firmly enough attached to be slid stiffly up and down. The rests should be painted, *not* left bright duralumin, otherwise much of the point of the exercise is lost. Incidentally, the best way to apply paint to duralumin is not to brush it on (eventually it flakes off) but to use an old glove and to *rub* it on very thinly, almost a smear. When this has dried, a second coat can them be applied with a brush.

BAIT BOXES

These are ideal not only for keeping livebaits fit and well, but for holding fish safely that are destined for transfer to another water. They should be roomy and *smooth inside* with no projecting nails, or splinters where the drill bits have gone through. It is best to make them floaters, because all boxes eventually become waterlogged and sink, although if dried out at the end of the season they will float again for most of the next.

63 A practical bait box.

Any soundly constructed box of some 18 in. square section and 2–3 ft long will do – or similar measurements. It may be necessary to nail some angle iron along a couple of the lower edges to stop the thing riding too high in the water. A slotted box with $\frac{1}{2}$ in. slits is preferred, but since most boxes come without slits, the alternative is to drill $\frac{1}{2}$ in. diameter holes over large areas, particularly at the estimated water level where the most oxygenated water can be expected to slop in and out. The lid of the box should be hinged and locked, as shown. It is amazing how often an open-topped box attracts predators such as herons, and how equally often an unlocked box attracts predators such as humans.

A word about siting the boxes. They should be placed over a clean bottom, gravel if possible, preferably with a foot or so of water below them, and it is better if they are in a sheltered bay or under a tree. You do not want them battered by big waves, or exposed to radiating cold during cloudless nights. The last problem can be alleviated by fixing a piece of polystyrene foam to the top of the box.

Other 'boxes' can be pressed into service, such as Woolworth's laundry baskets etc., but since you do not have to make these yourself, or modify them very much, they can be considered under the heading of the following sections.

WORMERY

Once again plastic rears its ugly head! Today there are short cuts to wormery construction: simply obtain a suitable plastic container, fill it with the appropriate secret compost, keep it moist, and add a lid to stop the worms crawling out. Brandlings are the easiest to keep, and they breed easily and often, but like all worms they go walkabout at intervals and you could lose the lot if a reasonable lid is not fitted. Our tanks are 2 ft by 3 ft and 9 or 10 in. deep. For worms in captivity we feel that a lighter soil, with plenty of peat, old manure, paper and damp sacking, is better than the heavy loam that they are quite happy in elsewhere. The best wormery we ever saw had a concrete base sloping gently towards a 3 ft high wall at the back, and in width was about 10 ft with 3 ft high walls at the ends. Manure of various types was stacked up the walls quite close to the top, but the worms never climbed out, nor did they come out over the concrete lip because it was always kept dry by a layer of polythene. This, of course, is merely a sophisticated version of the garden manure heap, and consequently not really suitable for lobworms. For lobs, a plastic or wooden box will be much better, and it is unrealistic to try to get them breeding: for this you would need quite a lot of boxes, some of which must be left undisturbed (apart from damping and feeding) for weeks on end. Feeding can be by various cooking waste (vegetables etc.) or by Quaker Oats. The latter was used exclusively by a real worm breeding expert we once knew. Nowadays we feed them groundbait and fruit waste (melons are excellent).

LIVEBAIT TANKS

Under this heading we will consider only modifications to essentially bought (or acquired) objects. Galvanised tanks can be used to hold baits very successfully, but they do *not* need coating with a liner as advocated by many anglers. Paint is expensive anyway, and if the fisherman really feels uneasy about galvanised metal he is advised to line his tank with a thin polythene sheet – the same system as can be used outdoors, with old boats and holes in the ground! (These make effective bait stores both quickly and efficiently, but it is sometimes difficult to persuade the family that they add to the attractions of the garden.) We have even seen a very successful storage container made by building a low wall (three or four bricks high) of uncemented bricks, forming a rectangular area of about 4 ft by 8 ft. This was simply set up on a lawn and polythene laid over it. In the summer the whole thing was dismantled and the grass allowed to recover.

With a galvanised tank it is quite easy to plumb in an outlet pipe so that water can be drained off and changed without, in fact, removing any fish. First position your tank so that it does not flood the house, then drill a hole about 2 in. above its base. The diameter of the hole will be determined by the size of the

64 A bait tank raised on a Dexion trolley.

65 Drain pipe for a bait tank (see text).

66 Feeder for bait tank, located in bathroom!

brass tap that you can obtain from the local plumber. Once the hole is drilled it is a straightforward job to fit the tap, incorporating waterproof washers. But it takes a bit of nerve to drill the hole in the first place, particularly if you have actually paid for the tank. Anglers lacking confidence have been known to have their tanks plumbed professionally, but this seems a little extreme and contrary to our principles!

LIVEBAIT BUCKETS

Gone are the days when anglers used patented, galvanised livebait buckets, complete with wire, lift out, liners. Nowadays plastic buckets with tight-fitting lids are used for transporting baits, and ordinary plastic household buckets for carrying them along the bank. But buckets can be usefully modified in various ways. The plastic lid can be cut away a little so that a Shakespeare aerator can be snugly fitted (Photo. 67) or the lid can be

67 Dustbin bait carrier with aerator clamped in position through cuts in the bin lid.

drilled with numerous holes so that the bucket can be sunk in the water and the bait left overnight. We should add that this is much better than keeping fish in keepnets, where they are vulnerable to the attacks of eels and pike.

All buckets should be painted a dark green or black: there is nothing more unsightly in angling than anglers carrying gaudy buckets around – buckets which, incidentally, have considerable fish-scaring qualities. A final mention should be made of polythene bags and their value for transporting fish. In the hands of careful anglers they are ideal, but in the hands of someone less adroit a puncture is almost inevitable. Barrie's first experience was also his last!

BARTLES' BASKET REPAIR

Bill Bartles, ex-England match squad member, first wrote about this in the *Sheffield Angling Telegraph* in March 1973 and in his book *Match Fishing Tactics and Baits*. We can vouch for its effectiveness: indeed, the job done by him in 1973 still survives intact today and in doing so surely outlives the whole life of many an angler's basket, for the trouble with wicker baskets is that the bottoms rot and fall out.

First you need a sheet of $\frac{1}{4}$ in. plywood with dimensions slightly greater than the outside dimensions of the base of the basket. Buy, in addition, the same number of rubber door stops, and screws, as your basket has legs. Then turn the basket upside down, take out the old bottom and cut back the ends of the legs so that they are flush with the rest of the basket. Now check that your bottomless basket is level.

Stand the basket the right way up on its new plywood base, position it sensibly, then carefully mark in the positions of the legs with a pencil. The next job is to drill screw-holes through the plywood in the centre of the leg positions, and slightly into the wood of the basket legs to give the screws a head start. Finally, turn the whole lot upside down and screw through the door stops, the plywood and into the legs. The new base can be water-proofed with some appropriate paint or polyurethane, and the basket can be immersed in water just as easily as with the old wickerwork when you begin (ab)using it again.

BROLLY LINERS

This is an item of tackle that you see in use in the bleak Fens and which, unlike the more robust brolly camps, is light enough to transport in the fishing box. The idea is to hang a curtain from the brolly struts using curtain hooks. Most of the latter tend to be rather open and they may need to be pressed close a little so that they get a wind-resistant grip on the struts. The dark green material we use is called curtain lining, and rufflette tape is sewn along both edges. This tape is designed to accept curtain hooks and is commonly used for suspending window curtains.

68 & 69 (Left) Brolly liner held with curtain rings on stays. (Right) Detail from Photo. 68.

For our purpose the tape along the bottom edge allows the material to be pegged down at the base.

The brolly liner does not need to be waterproof since it is light enough to dry easily and when in use will be in the vertical position anyway. Its main purpose is to add a little extra to the brolly's performance at keeping out the elements. In the wind, all brolly liners become of doubtful value if the brolly is set with the pole vertical and the umbrella part parallel to the ground, but there should be no need for a liner if the rain is coming down vertically! The trick is to set the brolly into the wind, at a fairly low angle to the ground as in Photo. 68, and then hang the liner round as much as is needed, weighing down the bottom of the curtain with all the items that you would normally have under the brolly. The curtain will always become a little grubby, but this hardly matters.

For a standard 48 in. umbrella a full curtain needs to be just over a yard wide and nearly 20 ft long, but at half this length they can still be quite useful although one cannot close off the front of the brolly with such a length.

Other materials can be used for the curtain but most have disadvantages which outweigh any advantages: canvas is nearly waterproof, but is too heavy; polythene is light but can be too light, or is difficult to fold if too thick.

ROLL-UP HOLDALL

It is fatal in angling matters to claim to be the inventor of any-thing. Nevertheless, our description of a roll-up holdall in *Fishing for Big Pike* received such a warm welcome in both pleasure fishing and match fishing circles that we can at least claim a measure of originality. Photo. 70 is almost self-explana-tory but several matters need *some* explanation. For example, the length and width is dictated by the tackle you wish to put into it. The length needs a 6 in. fold over at both ends, so if you intend housing 5 ft rod lengths you will need 6 ft 6 in. of canvas – to allow for shrinkage after the first soaking or two.

The canvas itself need not be very heavyweight material, for when rolled, and with umbrella and rods and rodrests and land-ing net handle inside, a considerably strength is achieved. Barrie's holdall is in the same weight canvas as used for haystack covers, but it could be half that weight without loss of value. The strap is of leather but a canvas strap (stronger than the hold-all) is far less extravagant. The tapes at the middle (see photo-graph) needed to hold the rods, need only be 6 in. long, but the tapes along one outside edge (three pairs: see photograph) should be at least 2½ ft long and 3 ft is not too much, simply because when rolled up and full of rods the circumference of the roll (diameter 9 in.) may well approach that length (allowing that a knot has to be tied).

The main problem with roll up holdalls concerns stitching. You would soon engage the wrath of the house females if you attempted to use an ordinary sewing machine. So unless you know someone with a heavy duty or commercial machine it is

70 Roll-up holdall for 5 ft rod blanks.

71 Detail of spool pockets at base of holdall.

necessary to cut all your component pieces and then have them stitched. The cost should be not much over £2: but if you have the whole thing made up from scratch the total cost could be well over £20. Buying you own materials and doing the job yourself should halve that figure.

DROGUES

For the angler who regularly fly fishes from the boats provided on our public reservoirs, an independent drogue of your own can be a great advantage. Most of the provided drogues are fixed amidships and this is not always the best place. With your own drogue more possibilities, and control of fly presentation, are in your hands.

Construction of a lightweight drogue that can be stored in your tackle bag is a straightforward task – with perhaps a little help from your wife and her sewing machine. The best

72 Simple drogue, made of plastic.

material is a waterproof nylon similar to that used in lightweight
waterproof clothing and brolly camps. Its proper title is Dun-
lopruffe 4 oz polyurethane-coated nylon. The reason for using
this material is that at the end of the day the water can be shaken
off and it can be packed away almost dry instead of a sopping
mess as would be the case with absorbent textiles. The material
can be bought from some camping and outdoor stores; we are
told that it is sold for making ground sheets and is available in
brown and olive green. You will need 1½ yards of material and,
given a choice, we suggest you choose the olive green. The first
job is to hem all edges with a ½ in. double-stitched hem. This
completed, turn in each corner towards the centre for a depth of
3 in. and sew down. These corners can be strengthened with
extra material if desired, e.g. canvas or leather oversewn to
them. Now find the centre of the partly completed drogue and
cut a hole of 6 in. diameter in it. Hem all round this hole.

We now have to make provision for attaching the cords to the
corners. The best way is to do this by placing an eyelet in the
turned down reinforced corner. Eyeleting kits can also be

obtained from outdoor and camping stores. The most suitable cord is sold in D.I.Y. shops for use with venetian blinds. It is white terylene cord of about ⅛ in. diameter. A 4 ft length is tied to each eyelet. These cords are now brought together and tied to a large swivel. The type we have in mind is a size 10/0 Berkeley swivel. This will be found in tackle shops selling a specialised range of heavy sea fishing tackle. To the other eye of the swivel attach approximately 5 yds of a slightly thicker nylon cord (¼ in. diam.) and this will terminate tied to the spring-type clip used on dog leads. This makes for quick, secure attachment to the moorings rigs generally fitted at the stem and bows of most boats.

BOAT SEATS

For the fly fisher regularly using boats it becomes a worthwhile task to make oneself a boat seat of some form. Several first-class D.I.Y. seats are possible, and below are listed some which you will find easy to construct with the minimum of tools and outlay.

The first and most widely used is the gunwhale board (previously used, when permitted, as a lee board for drift steering). This is simplicity itself to make; it rests across the gunwhale of the boat and so allows one to sit higher in the boat and thus reduces leg cramp. Its other advantage are in fish spotting and casting from this higher position. To make this you will need a piece of timber 5 ft long by 12 in. wide and at least 1 in. thick. This may have to be obtained as two 6 in. boards, but this does not matter. The next requirement is two pieces of 1½ in. or 2 in. square pieces of timber 12 in. long. The long plank is now placed on the bench (if using two pieces place these side by side with ends flush) and four $\frac{3}{16}$ in. holes are drilled 1 in. from the end of the plank starting 2 in. in from the long edge and spacing equally. This is repeated at the other end.

The eight holes are now all countersunk. Using 2 in. × no. 8 screws (brass if you want to prevent rusting) screw the two pieces of square timber under each end of the plank. These pieces then hook over the gunwhales of the boat and are placed in position where it fits tight across the boat.

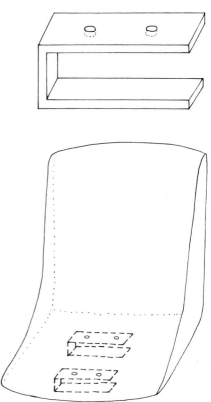

73 Basic stacking chair
(See also Fig. **I**).

Fig. **I** Stacking chair modification for boat fishing: slides sideways on boat seats. (Most boat seats have a 1 in. plank thickness.)

The next seat requires a little more work but should present few difficulties to the average handyman angler. The basic requirement is one of the fibre glass stacking chairs with metal legs – as commonly used in hospitals, lecture halls, waiting rooms and schools. It is sometimes possible to pick these up quite cheaply at furniture auctions. Having secured your chair the first job is to remove the four round-headed screws holding the legs, for the latter will be replaced by two metal brackets. These brackets are made from two pieces of $\frac{1}{4}$ in. × 1 in. mild steel bar, each measuring $26\frac{1}{2}$ in. in length. These are bent and drilled as shown in Fig. **I**. Prime and paint the brackets with a good metal paint and attach these to the seat by round-headed $\frac{1}{4}$ in. BSF screws which should not project from the under side of the top arm of the brackets. By now you will have gathered that the seat simply slips sideways on the existing boat seats. Its great advantage is that it is lightweight, waterproof and a great comfort to the back during a full day afloat. Les has been using a similar seat for five seasons and is very well pleased with it.

The third seat described seems to find favour with a number of boat regulars and is converted from a conventional typist's chair. (It is the chair which needs to be conventional!) It has one great advantage over the previously described seat in that it swivels – but it weighs a little more and the conversion is certainly more complex.

The type of chair to look for is the one with the central pillar coming from under the seat: this pillar is usually approximately $1\frac{1}{4}$ in. in diameter. Remove the seat portion, complete with the

Fig. **J** A sophisticated boat seat made from a typist's swivel chair. Fits any thickness of width of boat seat, and can usually be set bows-stern, or amidships facing port or starboard.

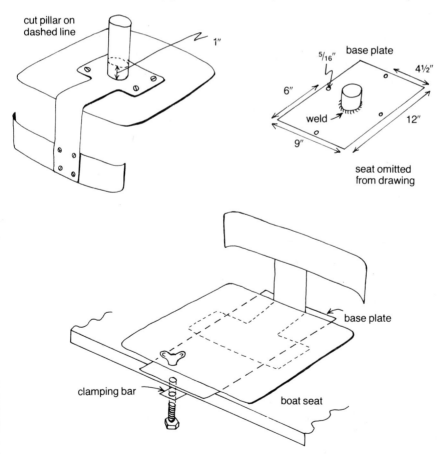

pillar, from the lower leg section. This is done by unscrewing the height-adjusting screw and lifting the seat section upwards. Discard the leg section, for which we have no further use. The next job is to cut the central pillar with a hacksaw to a length of about 1 in. from the seat. Make sure this cut is square. Next, obtain a piece of mild steel sheet $\frac{1}{8}$–$\frac{1}{4}$ in. thick and measuring 12 in. by 9 in.

At this point the work becomes a little more specialised, the first job being to drill the steel plate centrally with a hole to take the pillar of the chair *as a tight fit*. Four more $\frac{5}{16}$ in. holes are drilled, one hole per side (see Fig. **J**). These holes can either be tapped to take a $\frac{5}{16}$ in. by 2 in. machine screw or the screw can be left a loose fit. The first method is preferred, however, as it prevents loss.

The next task is the welding of the plate to the central pillar of the chair. Here it is suggested that the padded portion of the seat be removed as it makes the part needing the work more accessible. The pillar is pushed into the drilled hole in the centre of the plate, keeping flush with the underside. Take care when welding to keep the pillar in true upright position. The drawings should help to explain the procedures. You require the two end holes to match up if placed longwise on the plate and the two inner holes to match up if placed across the plate. The option is intended to take into account the variation in the width of boat seats. The final figure shows how the seat is fitted to the boat seat by means of the bar screwed up tight on the underside with the use of wing nuts.

We recognise the fact that the construction of this seat may be beyond the abilities of many of our readers, but if specialised help is available this is certainly a very worthwhile type of boat seat.

Finally, the cheapest and most comfortable seat of all is a part-inflated motor-scooter tyre inner tube. Barrie used one for a whole season, smugly aware of the fact that he was sitting on an additional flotation aid in the event of a disaster.

PART THREE

Fly fishing, flies, accessories and spinners and spoons

Fly fishing, flies and accessories

INTRODUCTION

In discussing fishing with anglers over the years, both at the waterside and in my position as a tackle dealer, one impression has come to the fore. This is that there is a considerable number of anglers who either prefer to make their own items of tackle or who seek to improve upon existing items on the market. With present inflationary trends continuing I can only see this number growing, and it is with this thought – plus the fact that I have always been one of the 'do-it-yourself' brigade – that I have put pen to paper. The ideas I have put forward include nothing revolutionary in terms of tackle; just ideas and items collected over the years which have given me extra pleasure in my fishing, plus the pleasure of making them, particularly the flies. No item is beyond the average angler in terms of skill; perhaps some of the equipment may cause a few problems, but none that cannot be overcome.

The fly tying section has been based on my experience over recent years in evening-class tuition. I found that a great many anglers believed fly tying to be some mystical and difficult art. By using the problems the members of my class brought to me, and resolving them in some sort of logical procedure, I was able to dispel this belief. I hope I may succeed in passing the same encouragement to you and to persuade you that fly tying is generally the mastery of a few basic techniques. I have arranged these techniques in a sequence to try and give interest and at the same time build up a useful selection of trout flies.

In the accessories section some readers may be disappointed at the omission of a portable rudder. The item was considered, but I felt that as most of the public waters are now banning its use its inclusion was unjustified. But omissions are inevitable

159

in any one man's 'anthology'. If the inclusions encourage you to take another look at your tackle; to seek ways of improving it, and to develop new ideas of your own, I will be content and your angling will benefit.

LES BEECROFT
Beecroft Tackle
Cherry Hinton Road, Cambridge

SHOOTING HEADS

Making your own shooting heads immediately gives the substantial advantage of tailoring them to your own individual needs. This need could be for a casting technique or a casting requirement, e.g. extra distance, or a situation where a long back cast is not possible. The other great advantage in making up shooting heads, or other lines for that matter, is that of making them to suit the requirements of a particular fishing situation. The situation I have in mind is that of an underwater weedbed or similar fish holding obstruction. When making up a sinking shooting head for this it would be possible to fit a short length of floating line to the tip to enable your fly or lure to fish closer to the obstruction with less risk of snagging. By doing the reverse, fitting a sinking section to a floating head, this again opens up further possibilities.

To be able to tailor lines to suit conditions and the tackle in your possession, it is necessary to understand some basic principles which must be followed. These concern the balance of the line to the rod, involving the AFTM rating numbers given to each. All fly lines manufactured today are given an AFTM rating number. This rating is based on the first 30 ft of line from the tip nearest the fly, whether it be a double taper, weight forward, shooting head or level fly line. You may also find that one manufacturer's lines may be thicker than another's for the same given rating, but the first 30 ft will always weigh the same. It is with this first 30 ft of fly line aerialised beyond the rod tip that the rod is said to be balanced if the line size and rod ratings are the same, e.g. a number 8 rod and number 8 line. Given this information, plus working on the basis that for every extra 6 ft of line aerialised we increase the line rating by one number, e.g. 36 ft of no. 8 line aerialised is equal to 30 ft of no. 9 or, *vice versa*, 24 ft of no. 9 line is equal to 30 ft of no. 8 line; with this information and understanding we can now go on to make up lines to suit our own needs. As each of us is an individual with his own casting style we find that some of us are capable of aerialising more line than others. This is largely due to good casting technique, achieving a high line speed, perhaps by the introduction of double haul casting. If you fall into this category I would suggest you experiment with longer heads of lower AFTM ratings, but if you have trouble aerialising line, experiment with shorter lengths of heavier line than the accepted 10 yard head length.

If all this technical jargon leaves you bewildered there is another way of finding head lengths to suit your style and ability. To do this you take the rod and line of your choice and commence casting, gradually aerialising more line until a point is reached where you feel the rod is working properly and you feel comfortable with that amount of line in the air. Now lay down the rod and cut the line at the rod tip. Join the piece outside the rod tip to some nylon monofil and you will have a shooting head matched to your tackle and your ability. It may be frowned upon by the technical wizards but it certainly works!

If when reading this you are new to shooting heads I would first suggest that your initial attempts are directed at some old double tapered lines. When all the principles are understood, start on your new line. It is of course of financial advantage at this stage if you have a friend doing the same thing, for then the cost of a double tapered line can be divided between you as each end provides one shooting head. Should this not be possible you will find that most good tackle shops specialising in game fishing will sell you half a line at half the cost of the double tapered line.

Having decided on the ultimate length of the head, using the previously gathered information, we come to the task of choosing some suitable backing line. The choice of backing has long been a source of discussion among fly fishermen but most come down in favour of nylon monofil in some shape or form. The object of the backing is to offer the least resistance to the rod rings in casting, allowing the head to be cast further distances than a full fly line which offers resistance in rod rings and a consequent

reduction in casting distance. If this line were very thin, resistance would be least – but it would also be weak and would tangle
easily. If you have never had a 'bird's nest' from nylon backing
you may take it from me that it should be avoided at all costs.
Obviously we must compromise between very thin and very thick
nylon and popular strengths seem to vary between 20 lb b.s.
and 30 lb b.s. depending on personal choice. The points to consider are that the nylon should be reasonably soft and it has to
have a low stretch factor. This is very important when trying to
set hooks at a distance. To combat the tangling bug manufacturers have provided us with flattened nylon ('Tapeworm'), oval
nylon ('Cobra') and both of these help. Before starting to fish
with a shooting head it pays to give the functioning length of
nylon (usually approx. 25 yds) a good stretching, and it also
helps handling to mount shooting heads on larger diameter reels.
Those of you who have old *Aerial, Speedia* or *Rapidex* centrepins
will know what I mean. For those of you wanting the latest in
backing there is now a braided monofil on the market (Shakespeare 5000) which I used during 1979 and found it to have several
advantages over others. For example, it has a low stretch, is
less prone to tangle – and is easy to sort out if it does. If greased,
it also floats well.

The next job is one of joining the line to the chosen backing.
The knots suitable are the nail knot, or needle knot, or by using
cast connecters or barbed eyes.

KNOTS AND LINE JOINING

Having given the reader some ideas on making his own shooting
heads and custom made fly lines, a few words on joining fly lines
to each other and to various backings would not go amiss
at this point. I will deal first with the most common join en-
countered: the shooting head to monofilament backing. This is
achieved by use of the *needle knot.*

The first thing to do is to prepare the end of the monofilament
backing by cutting it to a point with sharp scissors or a sharp
knife. If using the flattened type of monofilament it is better to
split it down the centre of its width for about $\frac{1}{2}$ in. and remove one
side. Point the remaining thin section. Pick up the shooting head

and, holding the back end of it in the left hand, take a needle in the right hand (a fly tying dubbing needle is first-class for this job) and push it up the centre of the shooting head for approximately $\frac{3}{8}$ in. This will be found easier if the shooting head is revolved on the needle at the same time. Push the needle point out of the side and through as far as possible to expand the hole. Leave the needle in this position for a few minutes, then withdraw it and quickly insert the end of the prepared monofilament in the hole and out of the side. Pull the nylon through for about 12–15 in.

Pick up a large-eyed darning needle and lay it alongside the fly line with the eye protruding beyond the cut end. Fold the length of backing pulled through the fly line back to form a small loop. Grip this loop, along with the needle and fly line, between the thumb and finger of the left hand. With the remaining end of the backing wind this in close touching turns round the needle and fly line, working back towards the cut end and the eye of the needle. Make sure at this stage that these turns will also cover the hole and the backing where it comes out of the side of the fly line. Take five complete turns and push the end of nylon through the eye of the needle. Hold the turns in place with the thumb and finger of the left hand. Withdraw the needle towards the left, pulling the end of the backing under the previous placed turns. Now, with the left thumb and finger still holding the turns in place, pull with right hand on the length of monofilament going to the reel. This has the effect of pulling into the knot the small loop folded back before we placed the turns around the fly line. With this slack taken up you can now carefully release your grip with the left hand and see if the band of nylon turns are positioned correctly. If they are not, now is the time to adjust them before final tightening. If all is satisfactory, pull on the reel line where it emerges from the centre of the fly line and also on the free end, thus tightening the knot. Cut off the free end of nylon close to the knot. To improve the knot still further the square cut end of the fly line can be tapered off carefully with sharp scissors, being careful of the backing line. The last $\frac{3}{4}$ in. of the line can now be given a coat of Vycoat which will give a smooth plastic type finish to the knot and greatly assist the passage of line through the rod rings during false casting.

With braided monofilament backing now gaining in popularity,

I have experimented with various methods of joining this to shooting heads and pass on the method I have found to be the most successful.

Braided monofilament, by its VEM construction, has a hollow centre. By pushing a large needle (I use a dart) up the centre of the backing it can be stretched open. It will fray a bit at the end but this does not matter at this stage. With the dart pushed up the backing for the length of the point (about $2\frac{1}{2}$ in.) I place this end in a boiling kettle for about 2–3 minutes before removing it and allowing it to cool. When cool I remove the dart, and this gives the backing an enlarged section at the end. By pointing up the end of the shooting head and with careful manipulation I thread the shooting head end down the centre of the backing to the full extent of the enlarged section. Having successfully reached this stage any frayed ends of the backing are trimmed off.

The next operation has to be done with great care. Using the new 'Super Glue' I squeeze this over the section of the backing with the fly line inside. Being very liquid it runs over the area quite well. The thing to ensure is that it gets to all parts. Hold free from any surplus while doing this and revolve the line backwards and forwards to get an even flow. Continue to hold until it sets. This is generally about one minute. (Although the makers claim the bond is ten seconds I have found it stays pliable but not sticky and dangerous for some five minutes.) This gives time for our next operation. Using the thinner gauge of rod-whipping silk the section we coated with glue is now whipped tightly and closely as if you were whipping a line splicing. This has to be done while the glue has this softness. If left for an hour or so it dries so hard it cuts the silk on the rough edges. The finished whipping is then coated with Vycoat. I have now used heads made by this method for nearly two seasons and so far have found no problems. The smooth finish it achieves certainly is noticeable on both the retrieve and casting when it comes into contact with the rod rings.

Our final reference in this section deals with a method used to join two pieces of fly line. By doing this you open up endless possibilities of creating lines to suit your own needs. A method I have used in the past is, I believe, the same as used by Dick Shrive, the well known Northampton fly fisherman.

Take your two pieces of fly line that are to be joined. The first job we have to do to each piece is to remove the plastic coating for approximately 1 in. in length. This can be done in two ways: either by scraping it from the braided core with a knife, or by dipping it into some cellulose thinner (acetone). Having removed the plastic, overlap the two ends of braided core. Using a fine needle and fine rod-whipping nylon sew these two pieces securely together. With this task completed, thoroughly coat the sewn section with Araldite Rapid glue. Leave for about 25 minutes, when the glue will be dry to the touch but not fully set. Again using rod-whipping silk whip the sewn and glued section and at the same time build up the thickness with successive layers of silk until it finishes the same thickness as the plastic coating on the untreated sections of the lines. When this level is reached, extend the area of whipping to the plastic covering of the lines for about $\frac{1}{2}$–$\frac{3}{4}$ in. at each end. Finish off the whipping and again coat with Vycoat.

Finally I will mention two other methods of joining lines and backing to line. These methods I personally look upon as something to use in case of emergency, but others may not agree. They are known as the Barbed Eye and the Cast Connecter.

The Barbed Eye is a small pointed piece of metal with an eye at one end and two barbs on the side of the shank. In fact it looks for size and all else like a straight eyed hook shank, pointed and barbed. This is inserted with the aid of a pair of pliers into the end of the fly line and the backing knotted into the ring with a tucked half blood knot. If you choose to use this method I would recommend whipping the section of fly line for the extent the barbed shank enters it.

Now to the second method; the Cast Connecter. This is a small manufactured item enabling either the backing or leader to be attached to the fly line quickly. Due to its bulk I have doubts about it travelling through the rod rings smoothly if called upon to do so (as, for example, in handling a fish with the leader longer than the rod, or large fish running further than the length of the fly line). The line is pushed into the end holes of the Cast Connecter and out through the centre hole. A simple overhand knot is then tied close to the end of the line. The line is now pulled, allowing the knot to be drawn into the enlarged centre hole but not out the end. The same procedure is now followed with the backing line at the opposite end of the Cast Connecter.

FLIES

Several basic patterns introduced in a step-by-step technique

To tie one's own flies must be the ambition of every angler interested in fly fishing, though some participants may be deterred by exaggerated accounts of the degree of manual dexterity required. But fly tying is a most pleasurable occupation and is not, as is so often believed, a tediously difficult extension of the sport. Many a winter's evening can be spent in creating a sufficient number of flies to see the angler through the next season, and the materials involved are small in amount and readily available.

In this section I will attempt to take the beginner through a short introduction to fly tying, using the basic techniques. These and the materials used will be dealt with in a logical step-by-step sequence and are within the limitations of any able-bodied angler. Master these basic techniques and you need feel no hesitation in attempting at a later date the creation of any fly or lure that you require.

TOOLS AND MATERIALS

The first essential requirements are the tools of the trade. Here again, from the practical angler's view, a number fall within the scope of D.I.Y., but you will need to buy a fly tyer's vice and here I suggest you choose carefully and remember that you pay for quality. A good vice will last many years and is well worth the initial outlay. One point to check at time of purchase is that the jaws close evenly and tightly.

The next tool that will make fly tying much easier is the bobbin holder. This small tool made from spring steel is used for holding the bobbin of silk. It enables the tyer to have both hands free for picking up materials without loosening tension.

The tool known as the hackle plier is the next to consider. Made from spring steel with two flat jaws, one covered with a rubber sleeve, its primary purpose is to grip the tips of the hackles to enable them to be wound round the hook much easier than by hand. This is one tool I would recommend the beginner to regard as an absolute necessity.

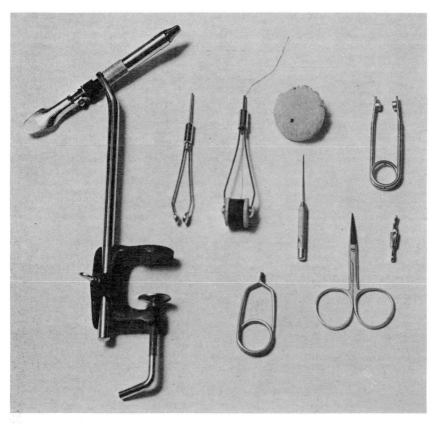

74 Basic tools of fly tying: on the left, vice; top row, from the left, bobbin holders without and with bobbin of tying silk; beeswax and dubbing needle; bobbin holder; bottom row are hackle pliers, cuticle scissors, and a tiny clamp for attaching to loose ends of silk.

A small pair of fine pointed cuticle scissors, with either straight or curved blades, whichever one finds more suitable, is another necessity. Next required is a dubbing needle. This we can make ourselves by quite simply pushing the eyed end of a medium sized drawing needle into a small piece of wooded dowel rod: about 3 in. of dowel will prove sufficient to provide a handle. A small hole drilled in the end will assist the job. The purpose of a dubbing needle with most fly tyers is that of placing small droplets of varnish on the silk whippings at the head of a finished fly, but more details of that later. This completes the list of essential tools:

1. Fly tyer's vice
2. Bobbin holder
3. Hackle pliers
4. Scissors
5. Dubbing needle

Desirable extras might include a piece of beeswax, some cellulose varnish (nail varnish) and a pair of tweezers. Another very useful extra item would be a piece of white card or similar material (approx. 10 in. × 8 in.) to place on the table underneath the vice. This enables the work in hand to be looked down upon against a white background, making for good visibility. A useful material clip can also be fitted to the jaws barrel of the vice to hold the small pieces of wire and feathers during tying operations. The one I have used for years now is a small piece (about 1 in. long) stretched around the vice. Pieces of material are now simply clipped into spirals and held away from the work until required.

Before embarking on tying our first fly I feel it would be wise to give the beginner a basic list of readily available materials that can be assembled at little or no cost. To aid this it helps greatly if one knows or befriends someone who shoots or lives in the country. But for townies like myself a visit to the local poulterer or butcher can be quite rewarding especially at Christmas time when all the pheasants, partridges, hares, etc. are in good stock. I have found a request in the form of telling him what you want and showing him some examples of the use to which you put them immediately gets his attention and usually a 'help yourself' reply. A list of materials to start the beginner off with some basic flies could read as follows.

Tying silk This comes in three grades which are identified as, firstly, Naples silk, (slightly the strongest and a good one to begin with): one reel each of black, olive and brown would cover most needs. The second grade, called Gossamer, is thinner than Naples and is mainly used when tying very small flies and nymphs where bulk is to be avoided. The last is Marabou Floss silk and this is used for building up bodies of some flies where bulk is required to be over covered. This silk comes in a 2-ply state and should be separated for use to ensure a flat, even covering.

Tinsels and Wires These are available in flat (various widths), round, and oval in section and usually in gold or silver colouring. The wider flat sections are used for making metal-bodied flies (Butcher) or for ribbing large lures. The smaller flat tinsels and the round and oval sections are almost exclusively used for 'ribbing'. Use the appropriate size for the fly being tied.

Varnish A clear cellulose varnish (nail varnish) used for sealing heads of flies when finished. Also available in black or red for heads of lures.

Wax Soft white palm wax to use for waxing tying silk to enable fur, wool, etc. to be dubbed to it. I do not recommend the use of liquid wax as this is messy and expensive.

Feathers and Fur
Cock and hen pheasant: centre tail feathers
Hen pheasant: wing quills
Mallard duck: bronze shoulder, silver breast and blue wing quill feathers
Partridge: shoulder and breast feathers, plus tail quills
Rabbit skin
Hare skin and ears
Peacock tail feathers
Swan quills (collected from shores of most public waters – can be dyed easily)
Ostrich
Squirrel tails (common grey) can be dyed black etc.
Chadwick wool (local haberdashery store – several colours available)
Raffene
Polythene sheet 150 gauge
Metallic sellotape, sweet wrappers, etc.

Good cock hackles for dressing some flies, especially dry flies, are best obtained from suppliers of fly tying materials. Feathers for tying streamer lures etc. are best obtained by buying a mixed packet of saddle hackles.

Before leaving materials, a brief word on storage: when storing all fur or feathers make sure everything is well treated with moth repellent (napthalene) and make sure any fur or skin obtained is thoroughly cleaned and dried out before storing. If one wants to obtain more information on treating and storing fly tying materials I would refer them to *Fly Tying Materials* by E. Lieshor. This is an American book available in this country and a wealth of information on treating all kinds of fur and feather is included.

Most materials can also be dyed various colours, providing it is darker than the original, by using household Dylon dyes highly concentrated. The secret of success here is to make sure that all materials are thoroughly de-greased by washing in hot (not boiling) water with plenty of detergent and then rinsing just as thoroughly. The other important thing about all materials when dyeing or washing is that at no time should the water or dye mixture be allowed to boil. Never apply too hot a source of artificial heat. If necessary, materials can be dried quickly with a hair drier. If not, I would suggest laying the material out on newspaper or towels and allowing it to dry naturally.

The last items required are, of course, hooks. Many words have been written on hooks and it is not the intention within this small section to repeat them. The main points I will stress are that you choose carefully. Here are a few points for guidance.

a) Open eyes – end result obvious.
b) Badly tempered – these will either break easily or bend, usually when a fly is nearly complete or worse still when a fish is hooked. Always check hooks in vice before commencing tying.
c) Barbs cut too deep – causes point to break off easily.
d) Points too long – difficult to get a hook hold behind the barb.
e) Up or down eyed? Personally I have no feelings either way; in fact I would be quite happy if they made them with straight eyes.

FIRST STEPS

With this list of materials we can now proceed to the practical part of the exercise. We start with what is known as running on the silk and the whip finish. These are the two basic points of all fly tying. Begin by placing your hook in the vice, eye pointing to the right. Make sure the point of the hook is completely masked (just) by the jaws of the vice. Screw the vice up tight and twang the hook to test the temper. Take up the bobbin holder loaded with a reel of silk and holding the free end of silk in the left hand, bobbin holder in the right, pass the silk across the top of the hook shank immediately behind the eye of the hook. Work the silk around the hook shank in a clockwise direction, angling the silk to the left with the bobbin holder. If done correctly this will tuck in the free end being held in the left hand.

Having achieved the catching in of the silk proceed with close butted turns of silk towards the bend of the hook. These close butted turns of silk applied with a tight even tension are the sound base of all flies and are important in that respect. To help one achieve the close butting easily without eye strain one should move the free end of silk in the left hand towards the left and hold it at a 45° angle above the hook shank. The succeeding turns of silk will now slide down this silk ramp to be closely butted together. One must avoid the tendency, in haste, to apply open spirals of silk as this will result in them loosening up later on and will be the cause of many flies falling apart. When the turns of silk have reached a point on the hook shank opposite the barb you now return the silk in the same close butted terms to the starting point. The shank is now covered with two layers of silk (which is sometimes sufficient for the bodies of some flies).

Having completed the first basic exercise we follow this with the whip finish. With the silk now at the eye of the hook, as would usually be the position if we were tying an actual fly, wind on enough turns to form a head of appropriate size to the hook size used. For those anglers familiar with rod making and whipping rod rings on, the whip finish should provide no problems. With a length of approximately 9 in., form this into a loop and lie the ends together. Lay this loop alongside the head of the fly, looped end protruding to the right beyond the eye of the hook. Wind 4–6 more turns round both the nylon loop and the head of the fly together. Cut off the silk, leaving approximately 3 in. of tail. Hold the silk tight at the fly head with a finger of the left hand pressed against the head of the fly. Place the free end of silk through the nylon loop and then withdraw the loop *towards the left*, thus pulling the free end of silk back under the last turns of silk. Pull the silk tightly to close up any loose turns and cut off close to the head of the fly. With the aid of the

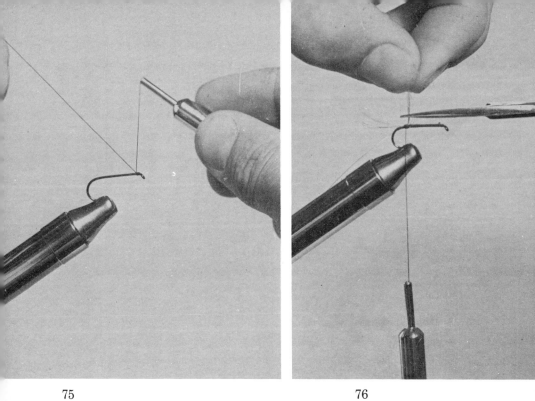

75

76

75–82 Basic steps in constructing a fly. As described in text.

77

78

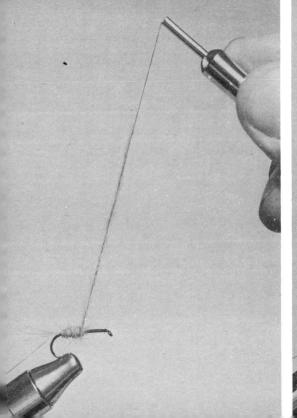

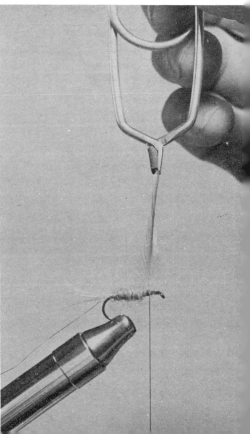

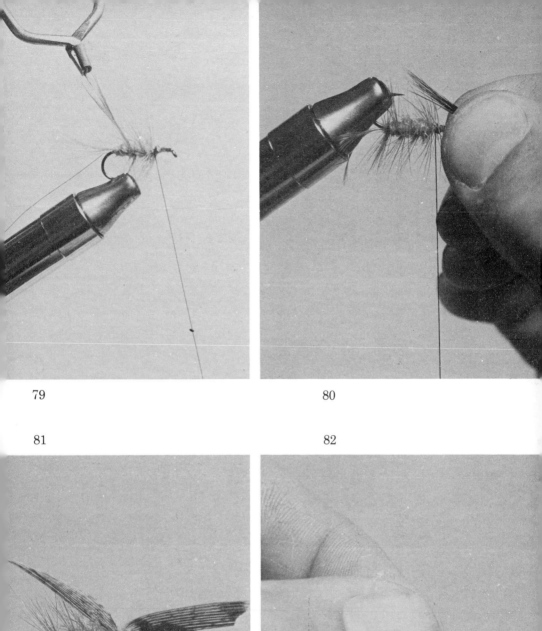

79

80

81

82

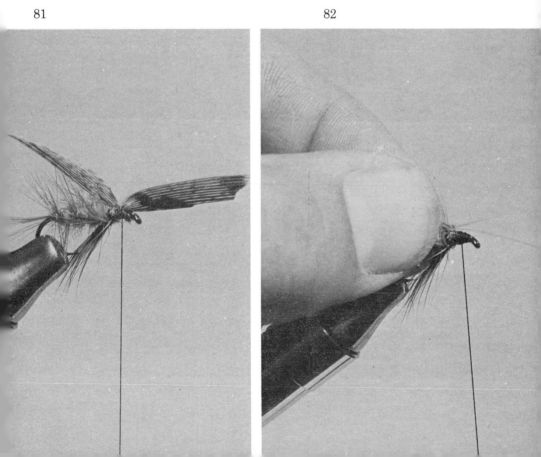

83 Constructing a fly: the final touch.

dubbing needle place a small droplet of cellulose varnish on the head of the fly and allow to dry.

Without having actually tied a fly we should now have achieved two important basic techniques; those of starting and finishing off a fly. With these mastered we can now proceed to tie some flies, using extra techniques which I shall introduce gradually. We will start with a simple hackled wet fly, namely, the 'Partridge and Orange'.

Partridge and Orange
Materials required:
Turn down eyed hook size 10, 12 or 14
Orange tying silk
1 brown partridge shoulder feather

Method: Run on the tying silk in close butted turns as described in the first exercise to a point opposite the barb of the hook, then return the silk in same close butted turns to a point approximately $\frac{1}{16}$ in. from the eye of the hook. Leave the silk hanging in the bobbin holder and take up the brown partridge hackle. On examining this it will be seen to have a distinct curve to the quill and at the lower end of the quill you will notice a small section of fluffy down-like feather. This will tear off, leaving only the actual feather fibres.

84 Partridge and Orange.

Having stripped off the 'flue', as it is called, hold the hackle stalk on edge between the thumb and finger of your left hand. With the point or quill of it curving towards the rear (bend) of the hook lay it on top of the hook shank, on edge, at the point where the silk is hanging. Now bring up the silk and take a turn over the hackle stalk towards the left. Bring the silk up again from the left-hand side of the stalk and cross over the stalk again, this time towards the right. Ensure that the hackle stalk stays on edge during this operation. Repeat these turns once more. This is what is referred to as the 'figure of eight' method of tying in. Bend the protruding butt end of hackle stalk (held in the left hand) to the left and take four or five more close turns round both the stalk and the hook, moving towards the left. Your silk should now be hanging at a point approx. $\frac{3}{16}$ in. back from the eye of the hook and about $\frac{1}{8}$ in. behind the tied-in hackle. Take up your hackle pliers and attach these carefully to the tip end of the centre quill of the hackle. With the aid of this little tool wind the hackle on edge for two or three complete turns side by side round the hook. These turns are towards the rear, to finish in line with the hanging silk. These turns will have the effect of opening up the feather fibres of the hackle to give it a 'sweep's brush' appearance as it is wound round the fly. With the hackle pliers still firmly clipped to the hackle tip move this slightly to the left with the left hand and with the right hand bring up the silk and take two turns over the hackle quill. Ensure all is secure and with the tips of the scissors cut off the remaining hackle tip close to fly body. Now move the silk in turns through the hackle fibres towards the front of the hackle. When this position is reached, with the silk build up a head for the fly and complete the whip finish as previously described. You should have now successfully completed your first fly. It should look like the fly in Photo. 84.

For our next exercise we will tie another hackle wet fly and this time we will add a further technique in building the body. The fly this time is known as the 'Black and Peacock Spider'. This fly is generally fished as an imitation of the freshwater snail and is a very useful fly to have in one's box.

Black and Peacock Spider
Materials required:
Turned down eyed (T.D.E.) hook size 8–10 or 12
Black tying silk
2 strands of peacock herl
9 in. black Marabou floss silk
1 black hen hackle

Method: Place the hook in the vice and run on the silk to bend of the hook as in the previous exercise. At this point leave the silk dangling in the bobbin holder. Take two pieces of peacock herl (these are the individual feather strands that make up the peacock's tail feathers) and holding these in the left hand offer the butt ends up to the hook shank where the silk is hanging, placing the ends under the hook shank from the front to lie against the left-hand side of the silk and protruding towards the operator by approximately ¼ in. Bring the silk up with the right hand and catch in these ends with 2–3 turns of silk. Fold these two strands to the left and tuck out of the way into the material clip on the vice. Return the silk to a point approximately $\frac{3}{16}$ in. from the eye. Take up the length of floss silk and twist the two strands apart. Take one strand and tie in where the silk is now hanging in same manner as the peacock herl was tied in at the rear. Leave the tying silk hanging at this point

85 Black and Peacock Spider.

and with the right hand take up the floss silk that is now hanging. By passing this from hand to hand wind this round the body of the fly, working backwards and forwards covering the tied-in ends of the peacock herl at the rear (when reached) and slightly thickening the body near the front. When the body has reached the required shape finish off with floss silk at the point where we tied it in, and tie it off in this position by holding the free end towards the hook eye and taking two turns with the tying silk over it. Cut off the waste end. Remove one peacock herl from the material clip and with same hand-to-hand technique wind this on its edge (causing the fibres to stick out, as with a hackle) up the body to the front of the body. Tie off here as with the floss silk previously. Repeat this operation with the second herl. With herls now wound and secured you should have a tapered fluffy body to your fly similar, if you like, to a bumble bee.

Move the tying silk now to a point $\frac{1}{16}$ in. behind the eye of the hook. Take up the black hen hackle and strip the 'flue' (as with the partridge hackle previously) from the base of its stem. With its curve towards the rear of the hook tie in, wind on, and tie off in exactly the same way as with the partridge hackle. The only difference is that due to the large size of hackle more than two turns can be taken. Finish off your fly with the same whip finish. With its head varnished the fly should now look as in Photo. 85.

Having successfully tied two examples of wet fly we will now attempt our first dry fly. The style we will tie here is known as a 'Hackled' dry fly as opposed to a 'Winged' dry fly. The pattern we will dress first is known as the 'Black Gnat'.

Black Gnat
Materials required:
Turned up eyed hook size 12 or smaller
Black tying silk
1 large black cock hackle (saddle)
1 black cock hackle to suit size of hook used.

Method: Run the silk to the bend of the hook as described in earlier exercises. When this point is reached, take up the large black cock hackle and tear off a small bunch of hackle fibres –

about six. These fibres are to form the tail and are used thus. Holding them by the butt end between the finger and thumb of the right hand, offer them up to the top of the hook shank so that the tips protrude beyond the bend of the hook by approximately $\frac{3}{8}$ in. With them held in this position grip the protruding tips with the finger and thumb of the left hand, at the same time keeping the bunch in position on top of the hook shank. Now bring up the tying silk and take two or three turns around the hook and hackle fibres without releasing your grip on the fibres at all. It will assist greatly if the silk is pulled back in between the finger and thumb of the left hand into a loop and then pulled downwards: this will help to keep the fibres on top of the hook shank. With these turns of silk tightly in place release the grip of the left hand. If done correctly the bunch of fibres should be on top of the shank with the tips extending approx. $\frac{3}{8}$ in. beyond the bend of the hook, the tying silk hanging from a position opposite the bend of the hook. The next move is to lift the tips of the hackle fibres up and place one turn of silk underneath them behind the other silk turns. This will have the effect of setting the tail fibres at an upward angle. Cut off the butt ends of the fibres as close to body as possible. Return the silk in close butted turns to approximately $\frac{3}{16}$ in. from the eye of the hook. When doing this, take a few extra turns of silk over the last $\frac{1}{8}$ in. of

86 Black Gnat.

the body, thus thickening slightly the section that will be immediately behind the hackle in the finished fly. Move the silk forwards now to approximately $\frac{1}{16}$ in. from the eye of the hook and leave the silk hanging. Take up the small black cock hackle. An immediate difference between this hackle and the ones previously used should now be apparent. The cock hackle will be seen to be much longer, thinner and comes to a sharp point at the tip. The other striking difference noticed will be that it is much stiffer in the fibre and is shiny on the outside. It is these assets that make it ideal for tying dry flies. The stiffness of the hackle fibres makes for good floatability in a dry fly. The hen hackles we have been using are much softer and are used where mobility is required, as in the throat hackles etc. of wet flies and nymphs.

Now we return to our Black Gnat. Remove the soft flue from the base of the cock hackle just as we did before when tying the Black and Peacock Spider. Tie in the hackle with the 'figure of eight' method. Wind in the hackle, using the hackle pliers and keeping all turns on edge and keeping each turn tight up against the last. This will give a tight, stiff hackle evenly spread around the hook shank when viewed from the front. Tie off your hackle tip close up against the body and work the silk forwards through the hackle. If one see-saws the silk backwards and forwards when making the turns, this prevents tying down any of the hackle fibres. With the silk now at the eye, build up a small head with silk, whip finish and varnish. The finished fly should appear as in Photo. 86.

To summarise, you have now learnt:
1. to make a plain silk bodied fly;
2. to make a herl body;
3. tying in of three different kinds of hackles.

We now move on to the next logical step, that of adding wings to our flies. To do this we will start with a tinsel bodied wet fly, namely, the 'Butcher'.

Butcher
Materials required:
Turned down eye hook size 8, 10, 12 or 14
Black tying silk
Flat silver tinsel
Scarlet feather fibres (ibis substitute)
Large black hen hackle
1 pair (1 left and 1 right) white tipped blue Mallard quills

Method: Run on the silk in close butted turns up to the bend of the hook. Take up the red ibis feather and cut off a small slip of approximately four fibres and tie this in as a tail, using the same technique as used for the previous exercise. The only difference is not to take the final turn of silk under the tail. Wind the silk forwards, tying down the butt ends of the fibres in doing so. When the silk is about $\frac{3}{16}$ in. from the eye, stop and tie in the piece of flat silver tinsel. You will find it helps to cut the end of the tinsel to a point and just catch this pointed piece in with the silk. This will avoid an ugly lump in the body. Leave the silk hanging at this position and wind on the tinsel towards the tail in slightly overlapping turns, taking it far enough to cover the turns of silk securing the tail. Having reached here, alter the angle of the tinsel to enable you to return to the starting point in the same close turns. By using two coverings of tinsel it

87 Butcher.

greatly assists the achievement of an even, parallel body. With tinsel now at the starting point, tie off securely with silk and trim off the waste closely. Now remove the hook from the vice and return it in an upside-down position. Take the black hen hackle and strip off a bunch of fibres, keeping them all of the same length and tips all level. Approximately 1 in. of one side of the hackle should give one the size of the bunch I have in mind. With the bunch held in the right hand place it in position on the underside of the hook where the body finishes and with the tips just brushing the hook point. Transfer the grip to the left hand and take two tight turns of silk over the hackle fibres, using the same technique as for the tail. Keep these two turns on top of the turns used to tie off the tinsel body. This ensures that the throat hackle is tied in at the correct position. With these two turns in place and keeping the tension on the tying silk, press down on these turns of silk with the thumb nail of your right hand. This has the effect of spreading the fibres into a fan shape. With this achieved take another two or three turns over the butt ends and cut off the surplus ends.

Return the hook to the correct position in the vice. The next operation is to put the wings on the fly, but before doing this it is important that a sound base for fixing them exists. Take a look now at the small section of the fly between the body and the eye of the hook. It is important that this is flat and even. If this is not the case, correct it by taking turns of silk to fill up any hollows. Having achieved this to your satisfaction take up one of the blue Mallard quills and remove a small piece by cutting close to the centre stem. This piece should be no more than $\frac{1}{4}$ in. in width if using a size 8 hook and less if using smaller hooks, and should come from the blue side of the feather. With this removed, lay it on the bench with the blue side downwards. Now remove an equal sized piece from the opposite feather and place this on top of first piece, blue side upwards. Pick up these two pieces as one, adjust if necessary so that the tips are level and the width is equal. Holding them by the butt end, offer them up on top of hook shank, positioning them so the furthermost tip of each is level with the tip of the tail. When satisfied with the position, change your grip to the left hand, this time supporting the two slips of feather in this arranged position all along the hook shank with the thumb and finger of the left hand. Keeping firm but not crushing pressure between the thumb and finger of your left hand, bring the silk up between the pad of the thumb and nearside of the wing. Throw a loop backward to give slack, then take the silk down between the far side of the wing and the finger pad. During this operation the pressure between thumb and finger is not released at all. The silk is now drawn down tight with the pressure maintained. This ensures that the fibres of the wing feather are compressed one on top of the other to keep the wing on an even keel. After this one turn do not be tempted to release the pressure, but repeat the above, taking two more turns. Now release your grip on the wings and if done correctly these should now be sitting squarely on top of the hook shank. Carefully cut off the waste ends of the wings and build up a head with tying silk. When doing this, ensure that no turns of silk go further back than the rear turn of silk that tied the wings on. If this is allowed to happen the wing will be rolled over and spoilt. With the head complete, whip finish and varnish. See Photo. 87 of finished fly for final appraisal.

To provide an extension to our tying techniques we will continue with a winged wet fly and tie an 'Invicta'. This will teach us to 'dubb' a body and 'Palmer' a hackle, in addition giving more practice at the techniques already learned.

Invicta
Materials required:
T.D.E. hook size 8, 10 or 12
Yellow tying silk
Yellow seal's fur
Blue jay wing feather
Hen pheasant centre tail feather
Small natural red game hackle
Golden pheasant crest feather
Oval gold tinsel size 14

Method: Run on the silk to the bend of the hook in the usual manner. With this position reached, tie in the piece of oval tinsel and tuck it away to the left in the material clip. The next operation is to fix the tail in position. Begin by selecting and removing a small bunch of fibres from the golden pheasant crest feather. Tie these in as a tail with the same technique as used when tying the Black Gnat. The tail should be approximately $\frac{3}{8}$–$\frac{1}{2}$ in. long and curve upwards. Golden pheasant crest feathers have a natural curve in them so when tying in take full advantage of this. With the silk now hanging at the tail end of the body thoroughly wax the next 3–4 in. of the tying silk. This waxing of the silk is important as we are about to learn a further technique, the spinning on the silk of some seal's fur.

This operation is referred to as 'dubbing' and it forms a length of silk similar in appearance to a piece of rough wool. To achieve this effect the bobbin holder is gripped with the left hand and the silk is kept taut. A small quantity of yellow seal's fur is pinched between the finger and thumb of the right hand. The emphasis here must be a 'small quantity', for the next move will be found difficult if too much fur is used at one time. With this small bunch of fur between the thumb and finger of the right hand, lift the thumb, leaving the fur resting on the pad of your first finger. Place this finger under the waxed section of silk held taut in the left hand, then bring the silk down on top of the fur and place the right thumb on top. The silk and fur are now rolled together between thumb and finger in one direction towards the right. Keep lifting the thumb and replacing and rolling to the right. This operation will spin the fur around the waxed silk to form the wool-like appearance. Continue adding and

88 Invicta.

rolling small quantities of fur until a length of spun fur reaches approximately 3–4 in. in length. To form the body of our fly this fur-dressed silk is now wound round the hook shank in close turns, working to a point approximately $\frac{1}{4}$ in. from the eye of the hook.

Select a red game hackle and, after removing the flue from the base, tie in an edge close up to the termination of the body. The next operation is that of 'winding' the hackle back down the body in open spirals. This is known as a 'Palmered' hackle.

Take your hackle pliers and clip them to the tip of the hackle. Wind the hackle, working towards the tail and in a clockwise direction, for about three or four open turns so that your remaining piece of hackle should now be at the tail end of the body. Holding this still with the hackle pliers in your left hand, take up with the right hand the piece of gold tinsel tied in earlier. Wind this tinsel, also in open turns, in a clockwise direction. This will be seen to cross the quill stems of the palmered hackle, tying it down securely. With this completed the tinsel should now lie in a position at the front of the body. Tie it off securely with tying silk and remove the loose end with scissors. Also clip off unused section (if any) of hackle at the tail end. This completes our body.

Remove and replace the hook upside down in the vice and select a bunch of fibres from the barred side of the blue jay feather. The fibres are now tied in as a throat hackle in exactly the same way as done for the throat hackle on the Butcher, tied previously. Return the hook to the correct position in the vice. For the wings of the Invicta we select a well marked section of the hen pheasant centre tail feather. From this we select two pieces (one from each side of the centre quill) approx. $\frac{3}{16}$ in. wide, and marry these back to back with their tips level. The prepared wing is now offered up in position, tips extending as far back as the tips of the tail. The wing is now tied down, using the instructions given for tying the wings to the Butcher. With wings satisfactorily tied on, complete the head of the fly and whip finish.

The next lesson in our fly tying school leads us to the 'Streamers' or, as more commonly known today, the 'Lures'. These have varying styles of winging such as Marabou, hair, hackle wings.

For this exercise we will tie three streamers using each of the above styles. The streamers chosen are 'Whisky Fly', 'Sweeney Todd' and 'White Lure'. We begin with the Whisky Fly, using the hackle wing technique.

Whisky Fly
Materials required:
Long shank T.D.E. hook size 8, 10 or 12
Wide gold tinsel
Scarlet DRF floss silk
4 hot orange cock hackles of matching size
1 large hot orange cock hackle
Red tying silk

Method: Place the selected hook in the vice and run on red tying silk to the bend of the hook. Take a length of scarlet DRF fluorescent floss silk and tie in at this point. Return the silk to $\frac{3}{16}$ in. from the hook eye. Point up the end and tie in a piece of wide flat gold tinsel. Wind the tinsel back along the body to the rear and back again, forming a tight even body. Tie off the tinsel at the front of the body and cut off the waste end. With the silk left hanging in this position, return your attention to the length of DRF floss left tied in at the rear. Take this up and wind a small band approximately $\frac{1}{8}$ in. wide at the rear of the body. This is known in fly tying terms as a tag. With this complete, continue

89 Whisky Fly.

with the scarlet floss down the body in open spiral about $\frac{1}{8}$ in. apart. When the tying silk is reached, tie off and remove the waste.

Reverse the hook in the vice and with fibres stripped from a large orange cock hackle tie in a false throat hackle in the now well tried manner. Replace the hook in its normal position in the vice. We now come to forming the wing and this is constructed of either two or four whole cock hackles. Personally, I prefer four and it will be this that I shall describe. Begin by taking two matching hackles and place them together back to back (shiny side outwards in both cases). Offer these up on top of the hook shank for sizing up. With tips extending approximately $\frac{1}{2}$ in. beyond the bend of hook, note where the front of the body ends. At this point, remove fibres from both sides of both hackle stems for about $\frac{1}{4}$ in. towards the base. Do not remove all fibres or soft flue at the base of the hackle at this stage. Now take up another hackle and place this alongside the two already in the hand. Again, shiny side out and about $\frac{1}{4}$ in. longer than those held in the hand. Repeat this with remaining hackle on the other side of the wing. You should now be holding four hackles together with the two shorter ones on the inside. Remove a small section of fibre from the two outside ones to correspond with that removed from the inner two. It will be seen now that the section of waste still remaining at the base of each hackle assists greatly in keeping them all in order. With them held together in this manner they are placed back on top of the hook shank. When positioned to your satisfaction, bring the silk up and tie down the four hackle stalks on top of the hook shank. During this operation hold the main part of the hackle wing with the thumb and finger of the left hand along their length, ensuring they stay on top of the hook shank. With the tying down of the hackle stalks move the silk in a forward direction to the eye of the hook. With this position reached, remove the waste flue from the ends of hackle then turn the stems back and wind the silk back over them. I prefer this method as it gives greater security to the wing. Now trim off any excess stalk, build up the head and whip finish. To complete the head of Whisky Fly finish off with red varnish.

To continue our streamer selection we turn to the 'Hair Wing' technique and the pattern chosen, 'Sweeney Todd'.

Sweeney Todd
Materials required:
Long shank TDE hook size 6, 8, 10 or 12
Silver oval tinsel
Black Marabou floss silk
Magenta DRF floss or wool
1 large scarlet cock hackle
Black squirrel tail

Method: Run on black tying silk to the bend of the hook and tie in a length of silver oval tinsel. Return the silk to a position approximately ⅜ in. from the hook eye. Take up a length of black floss silk and separate the two strands. Tie one of these in at this point and using close turns wind floss silk up and down the body to form a carrot-shaped body tapering to the rear, keeping it in proportion to the size of hook being used. Finish with floss silk at the front end of the body. Tie off with tying silk

90 Sweeney Todd.

and trim off the waste. Return your attention to the oval tinsel left at the rear. This is now brought up the body in open spirals working in an anti-clockwise direction. Tie off at the front of the body. Take up a piece of magenta floss or wool and tie this in close to the front of the body, then move the silk forward to $\frac{3}{16}$ in. from the eye. Wind the floss around the hook at this point, extending the body approximately $\frac{3}{16}$ in. with this magenta collar. With this complete, tie off with tying silk and reverse the hook in the vice. Using a bunch of fibres stripped from a large scarlet hackle tie in a false throat hackle as practised earlier. Return the hook to its normal position in the vice. Take up the black dyed squirrel tail and select a bunch proportionate to the hook size and cut off close to the skin. Grip the bunch of hair tightly between the thumb and finger of the left hand about $\frac{1}{2}$ in. from the cut end and with the thumb and finger of the right hand comb these cut ends to remove any short or soft under-body fur from the bunch. If you fail to do this you will never be able to make a hair wing stay on a fly very long.

With the wing suitably prepared the next section of tying silk must be waxed and for this we use black cobbler's wax, a very sticky preparation that grips hair like a vice and is ideal for this job. Having waxed the silk we place the bunch of hair on top of the hook shank and tie in as we would do a feather wing but with one very important exception. With three or four turns securing the bunch of hair the important difference is that we must now take at least two locking turns of silk round the hair only. To do this, simply lift the tips of the hair up to the vertical position and take these locking turns around the hair only, not the hook shank. Return the wing to its normal position and wind more turns back over these locking turns which will in effect set the wing in the required position. With the wing securely fixed, lift up the waste butt ends into the vertical position, place the scissor points flat against the turns holding the hair and trim off. Cut in this position you should get the cut ends of the wing to slope off nicely towards the eye of the hook. Continue to wind on tying silk to bind these ends down and at the same time create a slightly larger head than on a normal wet fly. When complete, whip finish and varnish first with clear cellulose varnish that soaks well in and then, to give it that nice glossy head, with black cellulose varnish.

For our final streamer we look at the White Lure and this time we use a Marabou wing.

White Lure
Materials required:
Long shank TDE hook size 6, 8, 10, or 12
6 in. length of white chenille
Flat silver tinsel size 3
Large white cock hackle
White turkey marabou feather

Method: With the hook fixed firmly in the vice run the silk to the bend of the hook. First tie in the length of flat silver tinsel and follow this with the length of white chenille. To tie in the chenille, pull the fluffy pile away from the end $\frac{1}{4}$ in. This will expose the centre thread of the chenille. By tying this centre thread in with tying silk it prevents a large lump at the rear of the body. With this successfully completed, wind the tying silk forward to approximately $\frac{1}{4}$ in. from the eye. Take up the chenille next and wind this forward on the hook shank in close touching turns to form a thick even body. Tie the chenille off at the front. Return to the flat tinsel and wind this in open spirals to the front of the body. Wind this tinsel in an anti-clockwise direction and tie off at the front of the body. Reverse the hook in the vice and tie in a bunch of white hackle fibres from the large white hackle or a false throat hackle, then return the hook to its correct position ready to receive the wing.

If we now take up the turkey marabou plume we will notice that this is a very soft feather made up of soft fluffy fibres. It is these fibres that will form the wing of our lure. The nearer the base of the feather the more fluffy it tends to be. It is from here that we take the best fibres for winging. These fluffy fibres are very mobile in the water and when the lure is drawn through the water they move in and out in a breathing action, adding greatly to the attraction of the lure. The fibres are torn from the centre quill in small bunches until a bunch is formed large enough to make a wing for the fly under construction. The size of the wing will tend to look quite large due to the fluffiness of the feather, but it goes quite thin when wet. Bear this in mind when sizing the wing. With a suitable bunch of feather in the left hand offer this up to the top of the hook shank, the ends of fibres extending approximately $\frac{1}{2}$ in. beyond the bend of the hook. Tie the bunch in at the head exactly as for any feather wing described earlier. Trim off waste butt ends, build up a slightly exaggerated head with tying silk, whip finish and varnish and complete the head with black varnish.

We have now completed our lesson on tying streamer flies using varying winging styles and materials. The type of wing that one chooses to use for a streamer is usually a matter of personal choice rather than staying rigidly to the accepted dressings. You may well choose to make your Sweeney Todd's with black marabou wings instead of the accepted hair wing and may equally prefer a Whisky Fly or White Lure with a hair wing. With a basic knowledge of the techniques used to tie in these materials, which we now have, I would give you every encouragement to experiment.

To continue our fly tying instruction we move next to the tying of nymphs. Some fly fishermen and fly dressers find this section most interesting and go to great lengths and experimentation to achieve life-like imitations of the nymphal stage of our trout flies. For the object of our exercise we will be tying three nymphs, namely, the 'Pheasant Tail Nymph', the 'Collyer Green Nymph' and the 'Black Buzzer' or chironomid pupae. We begin with the successful and most frequently used nymph.

Pheasant Tail Nymph
Materials required:
T.D.E. hook size 8, 10, 12 or 14
Fine copper wire
Cock pheasant centre tail feather
Brown tying silk

Method: Run on the silk to the bend of the hook and tie in a length of copper wire. Take up a cock pheasant tail feather and remove approximately six fibres as a bunch. Offer these up on top of the hook shank with tips extending as a tail approximately $\frac{3}{8}$ in. beyond the bend of the hook. Tie in while held in this position. With this operation successfully completed move the silk forward to approximately two-thirds the length of the hook shank. Leave the silk hanging at this point. Return to the bunch of tail feathers at the rear and wind these as one piece around the hook shank in close turns, working forward to the tying silk. This will give a slender insect-like body. When the tying silk is reached bring the butt ends up into a vertical position and tie off, ensuring that the butt ends stay on top of the hook shank. Do not cut off the surplus fibres. Now bring up the copper wire in open spirals and tie off in front of the lifted ends of the tail/ body fibres. Cut off the surplus wire. Select a further bunch of fibres from a pheasant tail and tie these in on top of the hook shank with tips extending over the eye of the hook approximately $\frac{1}{2}$ in. Using the butt ends of this bunch, wind round the hook shank to form a ball-shaped thorax in front of the butts of the body fibres and tie off at the front. Remove the surplus. Now with the finger and thumb of the left hand turn the tips of the fibres left protruding at the eye downwards and backwards under the hook shank to form a throat hackle. When positioned satisfactorily, wind two turns of silk round them and the hook, close to the eye of the hook, to set them.

Return your attention now to the ends of the fibres used for the body. With your right hand pull these forward together over the top of the thorax and tie down immediately behind the hook eye. This creates a striking resemblance to the wing case of the natural insect. Whip finish and varnish. When tying this

91 Pheasant Tail Nymph.

pattern on the larger hooks mentioned it may be found necessary to tie in more than one bunch of fibres for each operation as mentioned in the above exercise.

We continue our exercise with another nymph, namely, the Collyer Green Nymph, one of a series of four very useful general purpose nymphs; the other colours being brown, grey and black. All are tied using the same technique.

Collyer Green Nymph
Materials required:
T.D.E. hook size 10 or 12
Olive dyed swan herl
Gold fine wire
Olive ostrich herl

Method: Run on tying silk to the bend of the hook and tie in gold wire at this point. Select 4–6 fibres of olive swan herl, depending on hook size used. Tie these in by the tips, leaving approximately ¼ in. extending at the rear to act as a tail. Wind the tying silk forwards to approximately ¼ in. from the eye. Wind the remaining length of herls down the body in close touching turns, forming a thin velvety body. When the tying silk is reached, tie off the herls on top of the shank but do not cut off

92 Collyer Green Nymph.

the surplus. Now wind the gold wire down in open spiral (no more than four turns) and tie off at the same point. Take up one strand of olive ostrich herl and tie in on edge as one would do with a hackle. Tie this close up to the body but in front of the butt ends of the body herls that have been left intact. Wind the silk forward to a position first behind eye of the hook. Now take hold of the strand of ostrich herl and wind it forwards on edge exactly as a hackle, keeping the turns close together. Tie it off at the eye and remove the waste. Return to the butt ends of the body herls and pull these forward along the top of the hook and over the ostrich herl hackle. This causes the ostrich herl fibres to turn downwards and forms a wing case on top of the thorax. Tie off these butts securely at the eye, cut the waste off closely and whip finish. Varnish to complete.

To complete our Nymph section we now move on to one of the most common nymphs found in stillwaters, the chironomid pupae, more commonly known amongst anglers as the 'Buzzer'. Again this is a relatively easy pattern to tie and is useful in a variety of colours. Good colours to use for the body would be black, green, red, orange, olive, brown. We will, for our exercise, tie the most commonly used, namely the Black Buzzer.

Black Buzzer (Chironomid Pupae)
Materials required:
T.D.E. hook 8, 10, 12
Fine silver wire
Black swan herl
Strand of peacock herl
Large white cock hackle

Method: Place the hook in the vice and run on a few turns of silk, enough to catch in the free end of the silk (about 3–4 turns). From the large white cock hackle select a small bunch of fibres. These should be the longest available because we want them to reach the length of the hook shank and protrude about $\frac{1}{2}$ in. at the rear. Lay this bunch of fibres on top of the hook shank with the butt ends protruding over the eye of the hook approximately $\frac{1}{4}$ in. With them held in this position continue winding on tying silk towards the bend of the hook in close turns, tying the bunch of fibres down in doing so. Adjust the fibres with the left hand during this operation to ensure they are bound down on top of the hook shank and held together as a bunch. Instead of stopping tying silk at the usual position the silk is carried on to a point halfway round the bend of the hook. This gives the hook-shaped body so evident in the natural pupae. When this position is reached the tips of the white hackle fibres should be protruding for about ⅛ in. from the last turn of tying silk. At this point tie in first the piece of silver wire and secondly, by the tips, 3–4 fibres of black swan herl. Some anglers prefer to use varying materials for the bodies of these flies. Some common ones used are black floss silk, black wool, and black seal's fur. Personally, I prefer the swan herl as it gives a velvety appearance to the body. It also appears to have more mobility when in the water than the more solid materials. Use what you feel suits your theories best. With the wire and body material tied in, move the tying silk forward to ¼ in. from the eye. On the larger size hooks you may require to do this in two stages as you may find the need to tie in some more swan herl halfway up the body.

Having got the silk ¼ in. from the eye, wind on the chosen body material in close turns up to the tying silk. Tie off and remove the waste. Bring up the silver wire in a reverse direction spiral to the body material and tie off at the same point as the body material. Next, tie in at the same point a strand of peacock herl and then move the silk forward to a point where the white hackle fibres emerge from under the tying silk. Leave hanging at this point. Return to the peacock herl and wind a ball-shaped thorax,

93 Black Buzzer.

using up whole peacock herl and finishing up at the front. Bring up tying silk and tie off with two or three tight turns. Trim off any surplus herl. With the left hand grip the protruding butt ends of the hackle fibres at the eye of the hook and lift upwards and backwards. Hold in this position. With tying silk in the right hand, wind a small head in front of these fibres. As well as forming a head this will hold the hackle fibres in the upright position. Whip finish and varnish. Before removing the fly from the vice take the scissors and trim the white hackle fibres at the head horizontally to a length of approximately $\frac{1}{8}$ in. You have now completed the Buzzer and the nymph section of our programme.

In our final section we will cover some miscellaneous patterns that are commonly found in the present day trout fisher's fly box. We will start off with what must rate as one of the most successful lures of recent years, the 'Muddler Minnow'. Introduced into this country in the 1960s from North America it has accounted for a large number of trout since that time, and large trout too. Often considered by some to be very difficult to tie, but like most other things if a few basically important points are adhered to the problems can be overcome.

Muddler Minnow
Materials required:
Long shank T.D.E. hook size 4, 6, 8 or 10
Gold tinsel (wide)
Oak turkey wing or tail feather
Deer hair

Method: Place the hook in the vice and run on the silk *with one big difference this time*. Start the silk at a point approximately one-third the way down the hook shank; leave the front portion of the shank bare of silk. For the time being we concentrate our attention on the rear two-thirds of the hook. Run on the tying silk from this point to the normal position at the bend of the hook. Select two strips of turkey feathers of approximately $\frac{1}{8}$ in. width. Place these back to back and tie in as a tail as we did when tying the Butcher in our wet fly section. Wind the silk back to the starting point and tie in the flat gold tinsel. Wind this down to the tail and back again making a slim, even tinsel body. Select two more strips of turkey feathers approximately $\frac{1}{4}$ in. wide and place them back to back. These we now tie in at the front end of the body as a wing. The wing should extend as far back as the extremity of the tail. Some fly dressers prefer to tie in a small quantity of hair, as a wing, before tying in the turkey feather wing. For the sake of this exercise we are omitting the hair underwing. Whilst tying in the turkey feather wing, ensure that the silk turns are kept off the bare section of the hook shank.

With the wing tied in we come to the part that deters many a beginner from tying the Muddler: that of tying the head. The material we use for this is deer hair which is spun on to the bare section of the hook shank. This is how we do it. Cut off a bunch of deer hair from the skin, about $\frac{1}{8}$ in. in diameter. Hold this with the left-hand finger and thumb and place it on top of the hook shank with the butts pointing over the eye of the hook and positioned so that the end of the body is about halfway down the length of the bunch. Holding the bunch securely with the left hand, take two loose turns of silk around both it and the bare section of hook shank immediately in front of the body. With these two turns in place, pull tightly on the tying silk and at the

94 Muddler Minnow.

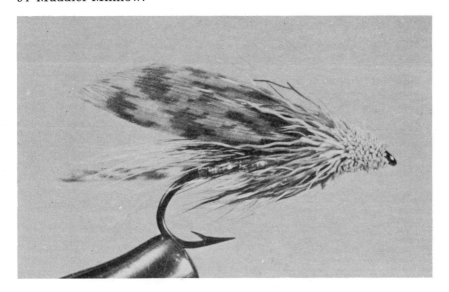

same time let go of the fibres in your left hand. By tightening the silk it will cause the ends of the deer hair to flare up and at the same time to spin round the hook shank. It should now look very similar to a hackle on a dry fly.

With the thumb and finger of your right hand push this hackle of hair back up tight against the body and wing roots. Compress the fibres with the left hand and take two tight turns of silk around the bare hook in front of the fibres. This will hold them in place. Cut another bunch of deer hair and complete the sequence all over again. In fact, cut more bunches and repeat as many times as possible until the bare section of the hook is covered by a tight stiff hackle of deer hair. Finish off now with a good whip finish.

Our remaining task now is to clip the hackle to the shape characteristic of the muddler head. This is generally either cone shaped or a round ball. The choice is yours. When clipping the head to shape leave some of the finer hairs at the back to extend like a ruff back over the front part of the wings and body. You should now have completed your first Muddler. I hope it has come up to expectations. One tip that may help with the head is this: it is far easier to build up a tight head with several small bunches of hair than two big ones.

For our next pattern we will take an easier dressing and some as yet unfamiliar materials. These materials we find in the 'Polystickle', a useful lure to have when fish are feeding on fry.

Polystickle
Materials required:
Long shank silver T.D.E. hook size 6 or 8
Black tying silk
Polythene sheet 100 g
Raffene (olive, brown or orange)
Red hackle
Red seal's fur

Method: Place the hook in the vice and tie in tying silk at the bend of the hook. *This is the reverse of what we normally do.* Secure silk with two or three more turns and cut off the free end. Take a piece of raffene approximately 3–4 in. long of the colour of your choice. Tie this on top of the hook shank at the same point, allowing about $\frac{3}{8}$ in. to protrude to the rear as a tail. Fold the other end back out of the way to allow work to continue on the body. Next, take the tying silk forwards in open turns to approximately $\frac{1}{8}$ in. from the hook eye. Take your polythene sheet and cut some narrow strips from it about $\frac{3}{16}$—$\frac{1}{4}$ in. wide. If you cut these with the grain of the sheet you will be able to pull in both ends and they will stretch down to approximately half the width. (If you cut across the grain it will break easily when trying to stretch.) When you have cut and stretched at least two strips of polythene, tie one of them in at the eye of the hook and wind on to the hook shank as you would do a piece of tinsel, stretching slightly as you do so.

Continue winding back and forth along the hook shank, building up a fish-shaped body. If you find your strip is running short, tie it off at the eye and tie in another and continue. Having reached the stage where you are intending to go down the hook and back once more, take a tiny pinch of red seal's fur and lay this on the underside of the body. Cover this with these last two layers of polythene. This has the appearance of a fish gut when finished. With the body having reached the desired shape, tie and trim off any surplus polythene. Reverse the hook in the vice and tie in a bunch of orange hackle fibres as a throat hackle in the well practised manner. Return the hook to the correct position in the vice.

95 Polystickle.

Our attention now returns to the strip of raffene. We must wet this thoroughly to stretch it along the top of the body to the hook eye. The raffene suitably wetted and stretched is tied in securely at the eye and a prominent head built up with tying silk. Whip finish and varnish, finishing off with black gloss varnish. The main point to remember is that it is no good tying in the raffene dry. If you do, when you come to use the Polystickle and put it in the water it will stretch. This causes the fly to loosen up and eventually fall apart. The last thing to do is to trim the tail square at its extremity and if opened up it will strongly resemble a fish tail. I think you will agree that it does fairly well as a small fish imitation. For the idea of using polythene and the creation of this pattern we must thank the inventive brain of Richard Walker.

We are now moving towards the end of our fly tying sessions and for the last two patterns we turn to two very important flies in the stillwater angler's repertoire. These are the Sedge flies and the Daddy Long Legs (Crane fly). We will deal first with the Sedge, and for this I have chosen again one of Richard Walker's dressings, the 'Cinnamon Sedge', the reason being that it shows us some more techniques in using the materials at our disposal.

The Cinnamon Sedge
Materials required:
T.D.E. long shank 8, 10 or 12 hook
DRF yellow fluorescent wool
Cinnamon ostrich herl (2 strands)
Ginger cock hackles (1 large, 2 medium)

Method: Wind on the tying silk to the bend of the hook in the accepted manner. Having reached this point, tie in a small piece of the yellow fluorescent wool and wind a small tag. Tie off the wool and trim the waste. Next take a strand of ostrich herl and tie this in close to the completed tag. Tie it in on edge as you would a hackle and follow it by tying in another strand alongside. Wind the tying silk forwards to approximately two-thirds the way along the hook shank and leave here. Return to the last tied-in ostrich herl and wind this on edge with close touching turns down the hook shank to the silk. Tie off and remove the surplus. Wind the remaining strand down the body working in close turns through the first layer. Tie off and remove the waste. Now with sharp scissors trim the body all round to approximately $\frac{1}{8}$ in. diameter. This will give a slender, velvety body much like the natural.

For the wing we use the large ginger cock hackle fibres. These are stripped off and held as a bunch of hair. Tie these in by the butt ends immediately in front of the body with the fibres laying low along the body. When securely tied in clip the tips off square with the end of the hook.

We now come to the front hackle. This time we use two, and use them like this. Having stripped the soft flue from the first one we move the tying silk forwards to approximately $\frac{1}{16}$ in. from the eye of the hook and tie this hackle in here. By bending the butt end of the hackle stalk backwards, after completing the figure of eight turns and binding this down, we have now moved our tying silk back to the base of the wing. Our second hackle is tied in at this position tight up against the base of the wing. One important difference in tying this hackle is that we put the outside of the hackle to the rear; the opposite way to the front hackle. Tie this in and leave the silk at the rear. Clip hackle

96 The Cinnamon
Sedge.

pliers on the front hackle and wind in close touching turns up to the rear hackle. Tie off and trim off stalk. Move the silk forwards through the hackle to the front. Clip hackle pliers on the rear hackle and wind forwards through the other hackle to the front. This achieves a nice thick stiff hackle. Whip finish and varnish. As the floatability of this fly is important I would suggest you now soak it in Permaflote and allow it to dry thoroughly before putting it in the fly box. When required at the water it will float perfectly without any further treatment.

We now come to the last fly in our collection and one I feel worth leaving until the last. This is the fly that gives me more satisfaction in tying, I think, than any other fly. To me a well tied 'Daddy Long Legs' is a thing of fly tying beauty. Let's see how we make out together and see if your attempts will give you similar impressions.

The Daddy Long Legs
Materials required:
T.D.E. long shank hook size 10
Cinnamon ostrich herl (2 strands)
Cock pheasant centre tail fibres
2 ginger cock hackles (medium)
2 honey coloured cock hackles

Method: Before placing our hook in the vice I suggest the first task be the making of the legs. Take eight single strands of cock pheasant centre tail feather. Tie in a single overhand knot in each one. These knots simulate the 'knees' and should be about one-third the way from the tip. Try and keep the knots the same distance from the tip on all legs! Place the legs to one side when completed.

Now place your hook in the vice and run on the silk down to the bend of the hook. Here tie in the two strands of ostrich herl as we did previously in the sedge fly. Wind these strands up the body to a point approximately $\frac{1}{4}$ in. from the eye, tie off and trim off the surplus. Trim the body herl as for the sedge to give the slim, velvety body.

Reverse the hook in the vice and pick up the eight prepared legs, making sure tips and knees are as level as possible. Tie

97 The Daddy Long Legs (viewed from below).

these by the butts to the underside of the hook at the end of the body, in the backward trailing position. Arrange them so that four trail to the right side and four to the left. Return the hook to the upright position. We now come to another new technique for you to learn. This is forming a 'hackle point' wing.

Take one of the honey coloured hackles and measuring from the tip about ¾ in. tear off all the fibres below this point. Prepare the other honey hackle likewise. Place these two hackles on top of each other, shiny side upwards. Place them flat on top of the hook shank, stalks pointing forwards over the hook eye. Tie them down with three turns of tying silk close up to the start of

98 The Daddy Long Legs (side view).

the fibres and halfway along the ¼ in. space left between the body
and the hook eye. With the hackles tied in this position pull the
top feather straight out to one side and likewise with the under
hackle to the opposite side. The wings should now be in position
similar to an aeroplane. Take two figure of eight turns between
them to fix them in this spent position. Move the silk forwards
to behind the eye.

Tie in one ginger cock hackle here and move the silk back
behind the wings to the termination of the body. Tie in the second
hackle. Wind the front hackle back, taking half the turns in
front of the wings and the other half behind. Tie off at the back

and move the silk forwards through the hackle and around the wings to the eye. Wind the rear hackle forwards through the other hackle. Again, half turns behind and half in front of the wings. Tie off at the eye and trim the waste. Whip finish and varnish. Remove from vice and I am sure you will be well pleased with your efforts.

Well, we have reached the end of our introductory course into fly tying. I hope you have found it helpful and instructive. If your efforts are giving personal satisfaction and the spur to go on and improve, then my efforts have been worthwhile. If this is the case I would suggest you enrol at a local evening centre offering fly tying on their curriculum or seek some personal tuition. It has been my experience in teaching fly tying that even the best written books are interpreted in various ways. Unless an angler is corrected early on he could go for years blithely assuming he had understood the book correctly! Do not be afraid to experiment with materials other than the ones prescribed. Do not fall into the trap of tying one of this and one of that. Decide on the patterns for the session and tie at least six of each. The fifth and sixth tied will usually be better than the first and second. Practice on one pattern until perfect. Good fishing!

ACCESSORIES FOR FLY TYERS

In this short section I look mainly at items of tackle available and offer some suggestions to improve them.

THE DUBBING NEEDLE

Whoever thought of this item must have had a corrugated table top. All my angling friends share my frustration; they put the thing down and it immediately rolls off the table. Cause? The round handle. To improve this item and remove this annoyance simply file a flat along the length of the handle. As this is quite an expensive item for its content why not make one? You can now eliminate the fault at the start.

The materials you require are an average sized darning needle and 2–3 in. of square alloy bar. Drill a hole suitable in diameter to accept the eye end of the needle up the centre of the alloy bar for approximately $\frac{3}{4}$ in. Fill the hole with Araldite or Super Glue and push the needle in. Allow to dry. This dubbing needle will always stay where you put it down.

MATERIAL CLIP

This is a very useful item for the fly tyer. The simplest and most efficient one was shown to me many years ago. It consisted of nothing more than $1\frac{1}{2}$ in. of $\frac{1}{4}$ in. diameter soft coil spring. The ends are brought together and hooked together using the cut ends. This forms a ring of spring which is simply pushed down the jaws of the vice.

MARROW SPOON

This is a must for the trout fisher and very simple to make. You will require a 12 in. length of $\frac{1}{2}$ in. or $\frac{5}{8}$ in. diameter alloy tube. The inside tube of some extending landing net handles is ideal. The other requirement is 6 to 8 rod handle corks with an internal bore to suit the tube used. Now you have the materials, here is what you do. Put the tube upright in a vice and with a hacksaw cut it down the centre for a length of 6 in. This done, remove one half by sawing across one section.

Having removed this section, clean off all rough edges with a fine file and round the corners and chamfer the front edges. The front spoon section can now be highly polished with metal polish to remove scratches etc. Now glue the bored corks to the remaining section, using Araldite. When the glue is set the corks can be sanded and shaped to personal choice. The one big advantage with this version is that if you drop it, it will float. This idea was prompted by bitter experiences with the marketed varieties, usually incorporating a priest, which sink rapidly!

FLY TYER'S CABINET

Keeping all the materials and bits and pieces associated with fly tying in a tidy and accessible manner often presents problems. I replaced the usual collection of cardboard boxes and biscuit tins with the type of cabinet described here. It immediately found favour with the people who saw it. So enthusiastic were their remarks that I have sold it in the shop for the last two years, very successfully (see Photo. 99).

The wood used is $\frac{3}{8}$ in. and $\frac{1}{4}$ in. Malayan plywood. This is a pinkish shade of wood that stains well to give an attractive finish. All joints are glued and pinned, and the inside of the drop-down front is covered with white Formica to allow it to be used as a work area, with a vice clamped to it. A small cabinet lock is fitted to the upper edge of the front cover and two screws are inserted into the bottom edge with the heads cut off. This provides two pegs which drop into corresponding holes in the base of the cabinet. These, with the lock, hold the front cover in place, preventing the drawers from coming out and also keeping one's materials secure. A suitcase type of handle is fitted to the top, and the whole project can be stained and varnished with

99 Les Beecroft's fly tying cabinet.

Ronseal or any similar preparation. To make a really pro-
fessional-looking job, all edges of plywood that would show can
be capped with strips of solid wood. Allowances in the measurements given below would have to be made if this was intended.
Materials cutting list (all measurements in inches):

Top $18 \times 8\frac{1}{2} \times \frac{3}{8}$

Bottom (as top)

Ends $11 \times 8\frac{1}{2} \times \frac{3}{8}$

Back $18 \times 11\frac{3}{4} \times \frac{1}{4}$

Loose front board $17 \times 11 \times \frac{3}{8}$

Long division $17 \times 7\frac{5}{8} \times \frac{1}{4}$

Short division $4 \times 7\frac{5}{8} \times \frac{3}{8}$.

Top small drawers (2) Front $8\frac{1}{4} \times 1\frac{5}{8} \times \frac{1}{4}$

Back $8\frac{1}{4} \times 1\frac{3}{8} \times \frac{1}{4}$

Sides $7 \times 1\frac{3}{4} \times \frac{1}{4}$

Base $8\frac{1}{4} \times 7\frac{1}{8} \times \frac{1}{4}$ Hardboard

Large bottom drawers (2) Front $17 \times 7\frac{1}{8} \times \frac{1}{8}$

Back $17 \times 3\frac{1}{4} \times \frac{1}{4}$

Sides $7 \times 3\frac{1}{4} \times \frac{1}{4}$

Base $17 \times 7\frac{1}{8} \times \frac{1}{8}$ Hardboard

Drawer Runners (6) $\frac{1}{4} \times \frac{1}{4}$ Hardwood

1 piece white Formica

1 small cabinet lock

1 carrying handle

Stain and varnish

SILK FLY LINES

Now that silk lines are no longer produced, those that are still
around have become worth their weight in gold. Although it can
be argued that the modern plastic line is superior in every way,
there is nothing to touch a silk line for suppleness and feel – as
every fly fisherman who has ever used one will admit, albeit
grudgingly.

Regular drying after use, and storing on a line winder during
the closed season so that air can circulate around each coil, will
help prolong the dressing and ultimately the life of a silk line –
but the two arch enemies, cracking through drying out, and

tackiness, are never far over the horizon. Often an old line suffering from these complaints can be picked up for a song, and it is worth the time and effort to cure them, even though success cannot always be guaranteed.

One school of thought on curing a dodgy silk line maintains that it is only possible by stripping all the old dressing from the silk by immersing it in a solvent (methylated spirit is ideal) then stretching it between posts in the garden and rubbing any remaining dressing off with a clean cloth. Once the line is dried out, it can be dipped into hot (but not boiling) raw linseed oil. The easiest way of doing this is to wind the line evenly along the length of a small bottle (splits from your local pub) that has a screw top. Fill the bottle with very warm water taking care not to spill any on the line itself, and immerse the whole thing into the pan of hot oil.

When the oil is cold remove the bottle, allowing the surplus to drip free, wash the line in warm water together with a little washing up liquid, then stretch it in the garden again and leave it to dry. Obviously a warm day is best – although the drying out may take a day or two in any case. Then repeat the process again. When the line has dried after the second application polish it with a small piece of chamois leather, adding a little oil to the leather if it begins to feel that the polishing process is 'pulling'. Leave the line to dry out for a day or so longer, and the job is done.

The other school of thought maintains that to disturb the original dressing is to court disaster. To prevent this the line is stretched out and alternately rubbed with a cloth soaked in raw linseed oil, then polished with a chamois leather. The whole process may take a week or so to do, but by doing the job this way, any bad patches in the dressing are built up without worries of weakening the silk underneath. Which of the two procedures to adopt must be dependent on the condition of the line.

Sticky lines are common and, short of stripping completely, the only cure that we know of is to remove the line from its reel, coil and tie it, then shake it up in a plastic bag into which a copious amount of Fuller's Earth has been placed. The line is left in it for a day or so, then stretched in the garden and polished with a cloth and more Fuller's Earth until it feels dry. Finally, a good polish is given with a piece of chamois leather. Some

100 Silk fly line held neatly with pipe cleaners.

anglers maintain that talcum powder is as good as the Fuller's Earth mixture – it is, we suppose, a matter of preference. We feel that Fuller's Earth gives a better finish and is less likely to clog.

Mention of coiling a line reminds us that it is imperative to use pipe cleaners with which to secure the coils – nylon line, pieces of string, lengths of wire etc. will all cut into the dressing and do more damage than bears thinking about. Photo. 00 shows the way it should be done.

Spinners, spoons and plugs

INTRODUCTION

Despite our enthusiasm to write this section on do-it-yourself items that it is possible to produce in the spinning and plug fishing line, it must be prefaced by a sensible examination of those things which cannot be produced by the average handyman, or, if they could be made, would not be worth the trouble and time involved.

Hooks, for example, both single and treble, naturally spring to mind. Most anglers have very fixed ideas on the type they use, and can advance a long list of reasons by which they convince themselves that they are the only ones worth using. Our object in this book is not to convince people that the particular type of hook we use is the best – but to assure anglers that regardless of the type selected by us, each is of the very best that has been made. We have carefully checked, and double checked each one to ensure that it is, and set out our check list here in order that it may be followed.

Here we are not knocking our friends, the tackle manufacturers, but we *are* suggesting that with modern mass production it is possible for the odd dud hook to slip through the system, and therefore one should be on guard to ensure that it does not finish up in the tackle box.

Temper is all-important – not ours, but rather that of the metal from which hooks are made. Each hook selected at the tackle shop should be carefully tested before leaving the premises, either by squeezing, or pulling the point towards and away from the shank. Those that are brittle will snap (yes, even with finger pressure) and those that are soft will become misshapen. We do know of anglers who take a pair of pliers with them and 'test to destruction' a hook from each batch that they

211

purchase. Their intention may be to test the temper of the metal, but we feel that there is some risk of revealing a weakness in the temper of the tackle dealer.

Barbs are next in line for examination, and any that are imperfectly formed join the rejects. We object to long barbs, and frequently reduce the standard size produced by the manufacturers with a fine file before actually fishing with them. But our largest collection of rejects contain those barbs which are too thick in the metal, and which would take enormous purchase on the strike to drive them home, more especially when using very light lines. Finally, the eye of the hook be examined, particularly in respect of the gap between the end of the shaped eye and the shank itself. Too large an opening here can cause the trace or line to slide around and come adrift. Usually we have a small squeeze at each eye with a pair of pliers before using the hook, not only to ensure that the gap is really as small as can be expected, but also to part test the temper.

Size of hook, type of metal (silver, bronze, etc.) size of gape – these are all matters of personal preference. As a generalisation we like our hooks rather wide at the gape, and made from the finest wire consistent with strength. Once selected and tested we store them in plastic or cardboard boxes, which are kept in the tackle cupboard. Tin boxes eventually lead to rust problems, whilst hooks carried loosely in any box and carted round by the angler in his fishing bag tend to blunten and tangle at an alarming rate. Fastidious? Yes, you are quite right, we are. But from long experience we have discovered that attention to detail makes for confident fishing and, more important, very few lost fish.

The final item in our hook section is a watchmaker's file and a carborundum stone. Both are essential for hook sharpening, and we take one or other with us so that hooks can be touched up at least once a day – more when we are repeatedly using a spinner.

We consider the mass-produced swivel to be one of the marvels of modern engineering. Try to make one yourself if you don't believe us! There are many different types on the market, all regarded by a remarkable number of anglers as indestructible, everlasting, and self-lubricating. Believe us, when we say that 'they ain't'. Swivels with a protective metal sleeve between the eyes, such as found on the plain bronze swivel, can be positive death traps of grit, weed, and moisture that spell out rust and wear. They should receive a spot of oil before they are first used, and be stored in a plastic envelope or dust-tight box in an effort to prevent dust and muck from the tackle bag getting into the works. After each use they should be washed out in a little petrol (lighter fuel is ideal) and oiled again. Watch for weed jammed at the base of the eye, or the junction with the metal body, and be prepared to ease this out with the point of a pin.

Although ball-bearing swivels are initially more expensive than the plain barrel, we believe them to be worth the extra cash – if only because the innards are firmly sealed, and protected from water and grit. We also favour the diamond type of swivel where there is just one rivet joining the two moving parts. This arrangement allows the joint to be inspected at any time, besides offering no 'catch' points where dirt can be trapped.

Link swivels can be a curse. Those of the split ring type will often allow the lure which they are securing to slide into one end of the link, and from there it is a matter of seconds before the lure is slipped and lost. Those with a safety-pin type of fastening are better, but need careful examination to ensure that the metal pin fits well back into the lip of the fastener itself. Those that do not fit securely will pull apart and separate immediately any firm pressure is brought to bear.

Split rings, sometimes used to secure plug bodies, nose fastenings on spinners, etc. together, are an evil, and often, unfortunately a necessary one. As we described in the paragraph on link swivels the ends of the split ring often open, allowing the item held by it to part company with the line. The answer to the problem? Well, we have now taken to opening each end on the ring and dabbing a little Araldite under the opened parts before allowing them to snap back into place. This is a certain cure, but not so final that a worn piece of tackle cannot be removed after a knife blade is inserted into the split ring to break it apart. Sealing the ends with a blob of solder is a definite all time cure for line slip, but this really is irreversible – at least, on the bankside.

The final item that the angler will be unable to manufacture for himself is Alasticum wire or similar cabled wire. It can be purchased in varying breaking strains from the tackle shop, together with cabled Alasticum. This latter commodity is less prone to kinking than the plain, single wire, and, in our experience, easier to work with. Manufacturing one's own cabled Alasticum is simple, and a large number of anglers (for a variety of reasons) prefer to make their own.

Start by pulling a long length of Alasticum in the required breaking strain from the spool, and fold it so that there are three equal lengths. Now clamp one end, with its three lengths, firmly with a hand vice or pair of artery forceps, and secure it. At the other end attach a weight with which to spin the cable together. The method is simple – one operator stands at the top of the stairs holding the clamped cable, and the weighted end is allowed to drop down through the stair well. The second operator then slowly and carefully spins the weight, layering the cable together.

The best way to spin the cable where only one operator is available is to fix one end into a vice, then, with a small dowel piece, wedge the other ends into the chuck of a small hand drill. One has only to turn the handle of the drill slowly and the strands will bind together evenly. Above all, when turning Alasticum, avoid over-tightening. This will stretch, strain, and weaken the finished cable, besides forcing it into kinks that are impossible to straighten out. Once twisted the cable can be cut into suitable working lengths (say 18 inches) or coiled loosely and bagged ready for future use. By choosing some of the very fine single strand wires available at good ironmongery shops, it is possible to prepare your own traces for fine tackle spinning as well as for heavyweight piking or sea fishing.

SPINNERS

One single word that covers a multitude of lures, most, if not all of which can be made by the angler. More and more spinning men are taking to making their own lures – in fact, we think that if prices continue to rise as quickly as they are today, we shall find the spinning man passing round his box of home-made lures for admiration in much the same way that the purist fly fisherman presents his box of home-tied insect imitations.

This parallel between the fly fisherman – especially the reservoir lure man – and the spinning angler is no light jest. Both, when one considers the retrieve of the line through the water, are basically presenting a moving lure to a fish. In fact we know several died-in-the-wool fly men who, when approached, have produced for us some pretty life-like near-spinners and mini-plugs tied out of fur and hair.

FLY SPOONS

Probably one of the oldest artificial lures of all, and a proven fish killer. They take about ten minutes to produce, and cost a matter of pence each. Start with a swivel, and mount on this a split ring. Next attach a long shanked single hook to the split ring, and the body section is complete. Now, from a sheet of alloy or tin, cut out an oval shaped piece and drill a hole into one corner of this. Carefully file the point off the end of a 4 or 6 in. nail; this makes a punch that can be used to tap a dish, or saucer shape, in the centre of the blade, assisting it to revolve when drawn through the water. The blade is now mounted on the split ring via the hole already made, and the job is done.

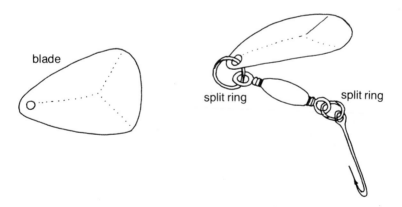

Fig. **K** Fly spoon construction: an old cold chisel can be used to impart the tripartite 'dents' ; hooks can be single or small treble.

Numerous variations present themselves with this type of lure. Whilst most of the shop bought items are very small, ostensibly to allow their use with a fly rod, there is no reason why they should not be scaled up in size, the blade itself being painted with bars, stripes, spots, etc. and, where needed, a treble hook replacing the long-shanked single.

A variation on the fly spoon lure is to use thin plastic sheeting in various colours for the vane. This cuts very easily, and when heated, using hot water and a pair of pliers, can be bent into any shape imaginable. Although the professional spoon is invariably round or three cornered in shape, we have had success with squares, oblongs, etc. which never adapted to a pure spin at all during the retrieve – just an occasional lurch and swing round the 'body', but which worked quite well.

Some anglers prefer the hook to be adorned with a tag of red wool whipped on the shank of the hook, or use a winding of silk and fur to produce an imitation fly, usually an Alder or Palmer variety. The permutations are endless, but we would add a caution that wool-type bodies tied to the hook should be thoroughly dried before being stowed away, otherwise rust, the great enemy, will set in.

DEVON MINNOWS

Another time honoured lure that can be produced at home. The possible exception is the metal Devon, needed for very fast waters where the lure must sink immediately to the bottom. Unfortunately the angler without a lathe, or access to one, will have to be content with buying these, or better still, reaching a compromise with Devons made from a lighter material such as wood, which can be fished with lead applied on the trace, above the lure itself, or in paternoster style.

Occasionally one sees advertisements for wooden Devon shells in the angling press, and these only need painting and fitting out with a suitable mount before they are ready for use. They represent fair value for money, and the answer to the angler who cannot use, or does not possess a lathe. Yet another type of Devon in shell form is the Dibro range, again frequently advertised in the angling press. These are excellent heavy plastic shells, ready moulded with fins attached and in a variety of sizes, that only need painting. It is also possible to obtain a kit from the manufacturers which includes transfers for the eyes, paints, etc. and with a little homework in a quiet corner, plus a supply of mounts, a series of lures can be made up in an evening or so.

Of course, the clever handyman can turn Devons out of a length of dowelling by hand – but it is a tedious business, especcially when it comes to boring the central hole along the length of the body. We have a special long bit prepared for just this task, and it is also useful for drilling similar holes along the length of plug bodies. If you must try it, remember to shape as much of the body as possible on the end of a length of dowelling which is easy to hold; the near-finished body can be cut free when the bulk of the work is done.

We discovered a reasonably cheap source of Devon bodies whilst we were float making. The balsa wood bodies for some of the duckers and zoomers are an ideal shape for a Devon, being further blessed with a very large hole through their centre. We dip them into very thin cellulose varnish, then hang them to dry, taking care that the hole itself is well filled. Any blockages can be cleared with a hand drill or fine rat-tailed file when the dope is dry. This seals the wood, and the next step in production can be carried out. Small D-shaped vanes are cut from sheet acetate or thin plastic, and a curve is cut back into the upright of the 'D' itself (see Fig. L). Now two small saw cuts from a small fine-toothed hacksaw are made at opposing diagonals either side of what will be the head end of the shell.

A little quick drying Araldite will hold each plastic vane in place within the saw cuts, and also allow last-minute adjustments to be carried out which will ensure that each vane is correctly angled. The minnow is now ready for painting.

Painting Devons – especially the small ones – can be a messy business. We have discovered that painting in the vertical position is easier than laying each object flat on the bench and then attempting to colour it. To assist in this vertical approach a small rack was made, consisting of a flat piece of wood 12 × 3 in. into which holes were bored at 2-in. intervals, and a short length of $\frac{1}{4}$ in. dowelling tapered at one end only, was glued into each

hole so that the point mounted upwards. When we have a painting session each shell is pushed on the end of a dowelling mount,
where it wedges firmly, leaving us with both hands free to work.
Nails can, of course, be used instead of dowel rod.

Most good quality gloss paints will produce excellent results,
but we find that the small tins of oil-based enamel, sold in model
shops for use on plastic kits, to be the best. To help in obtaining
a straight line where a two-tone colour is needed, cut and stick
a thin strip of sellotape along the length of the body at the halfway line. Brush marks that slip will settle on the sellotape,
which can be peeled off when the paint is dry, leaving a dead
straight line. The process is repeated, of course, when the
reverse half is painted.

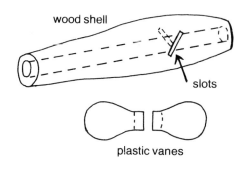

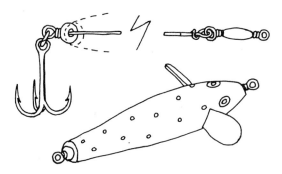

Fig. L Devon minnow construction: all dimensions and body materials
can be varied; slots in the shell should be made a *loose* fit and ample
glue used partly as a filler.

101 Balsa float bodies, showing their ease of conversion into Devon minnows.

Gradual merging of body colours, as opposed to straight lines, can be achieved with small cans of spray paint – the sort sold as touch-up colours for cars. This is where the painting rack is especially useful, and one merely needs a corner of a shed or room where the job can be carried out without damage to surrounding fitments.

We rig up a cloth background, stand the rack with fitted shells on an old newspaper, and then spray up and down the rack taking care to keep the aerosol tin at right-angles to the bodies. When the paint is dry, the rack is turned completely round, and the following colour is sprayed in – taking care to overlap slightly this colour on the previous one. Very professional results can be obtained quite quickly by this method. Our only word of caution would be to make sure that the spraying is done in a warm temperature, since working in the cold can make the spray rather lumpy. And, of course, do remember that the paint spray is a fire hazard, so no naked lights anywhere whilst work is in progress. Spraying through a gauze can produce nice scale finishes.

Mounts for Devon minnows should be good and stout. Not because they will be subjected to enormous strain, but because thin mounts will bend and kink during the casting process, effectively killing all spinning action. We use cabled Alasticum made from three 14 lb b.s. strands, and cut 6 in. lengths off the roll, enough for each mount.

At one end of this length a treble hook is whipped, the hook size in keeping with the size of Devon that it is going to support. If eyed trebles are used, it is essential that the securing turns round the main trace are kept as small as possible, and tight up against the eye itself. If this is not done, trouble will be met when the minnow is mounted – it will lie too far back from the hook, and lose some of its hooking potential when the strike is made.

A neater, and more effective method is to use tapered trebles instead of those with an eye. These can be purchased from a tackle dealer, and merely require whipping to the trace. The end of the trace is folded back under the bend of one of the hooks, so that both lengths of wire lie along the tapered shank. The short end is twisted two or three times around the shank and whipped into place with a length of strong fuse wire, finished off by the West Country whipping method (the same, in fact, that is used to fasten rod whippings). Both whipping and shank are now coated with Araldite and any waste trimmed off.

A plastic bead (again, supplied by the tackle shop) is slid down the trace and butted against the hook. This will provide a block against which the minnow will rest, and ensure that it can turn smoothly. Now the minnow is passed down the trace, and a small swivel is threaded on it. It is important that this swivel is small enough to pass through the body of the minnow if you want the whole lure to break apart, allowing the various items to be stored separately. We have never quite understood the logic of this separation fag that seems to be insisted on by the manufacturers – we use a fair-sized swivel, and prefer to leave each Devon ready set up, thus avoiding the fumbling required to match various sizes of mount to the correct size of Devon body on a cold day. Allow a $\frac{1}{2}$ in. of space between the end of the body and the eye of the swivel, secure with a twist finish and a little Araldite, cut off the waste Alasticum – and the mount is made.

THE QUILL MINNOW

Another of those small and very killing lures that has, alas, nearly disappeared from the catalogues in its original form. In the traditional model the thick end of a swan's quill was cut, sliced at the head into a 'V' into which was mounted both lead and spinning vane. Two sets of flying trebles on either side completed the lure, which was painted much in the same way as the Devon type. Today the quill minnow may still be purchased from the tackle shop, but with the body moulded from plastic.

Most of the lures discussed so far have had the 'easy' tag attached to the construction stages. We would be less than honest to suggest that the quill minnow is an easy spinner to produce, but, nevertheless, it repays both time and bad language that will be expended by being a splendid fish taker.

The problems of producing a quill minnow centre around its head, which in the professional model has a specially constructed spinning vane-cum-swivel made in one piece from metal. The nearest approach the amateur can get to this is by making a scaled down (very small) spinning vane as we outlined for the deadbait spinning mount. Instead of working with copper wire, use a suitable length of cabled Alasticum with which to bind swivel and vane together, twisting up tightly and coating the twist joint with Araldite.

Take a large swan quill, and cut off the blunt end. It is impossible to say 'cut off two or three inches' – the length of the lure will be governed by the diameter of the quill itself. Make a sensible judgment, and allow at least half an inch more than you think will be required. This extra length will be taken up with the deep 'V'-shape that must be cut to accommodate the spinning vane.

When this is done pierce a hole at the end of the quill, thread the loose end of the trace bearing the spinning vane through it, and pull the vane firmly down into the V-cut. There should be enough quill overhanging the vane to allow the ends to be bound together without obstructing the swivel in any way.

The final stage of construction is to whip a tapered treble of suitable size to the tail end of trace protruding through the end of the quill. Next, a length of cabled Alasticum $2\frac{1}{2}$ times the length of the body is half-hitched through the eye of the swivel, and to each end of this a tapered treble can be whipped.

Some professional lures are produced with umpteen trebles mounted on these flying traces so that they look rather like Christmas trees. We think two trebles quite enough, more than this adding to the lure's ability to catch on weed and underwater obstruction without assisting in any way towards improving its hooking potential in the fish's mouth.

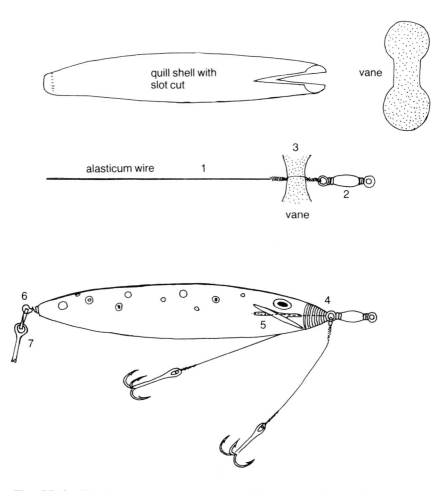

Fig. **M** Quill minnow construction: 1. Wire to go through middle of lure; 2. Swivel; 3. Metal vane held in position across its equator by twisted wire; 4. Slot closed over vane and bound with whipping silk; 5. Vane with blades now bent at opposing angles (equator horizontal still); 6. Terminal loop in wire attached by split ring to treble (7).

Those anglers who need a well-weighted quill should add dust shot or lead wire into the body when the trace has been threaded through the end hole of the quill, but before the vane is finally secured into place and bound up. The last task is that of painting and this has to be done 'on the flat', with the lure lying on the bench. Start by spreading a little turpentine on a cloth, and use this to remove the natural oil that is on the body of the quill, allowing the paint to grip. It pays to take a little time with the brush work, concentrating on natural colours and a bar effect (rather like the flanks on a perch) rather than trying to paint a picture-book fish. Eyes can be added – though for what purpose we fail to see. Spinners catch fish equally well without them.

SPOONS

Talk of spinning or spinning lures and the mental picture that will flash through most people's minds is that of a spoon. Somehow, the spoon is synonymous with spinning – and why not? It has been responsible for the capture of just about every species of fish swimming, from the mighty Mahseer of India to the nine-inch jack of an English pond. Somehow this spoon bait – a good hefty one, or even a tiny one-inch model – seems to embody confidence that need not necessarily stem from its use; just to know that there is one in the lure box can be sufficient to add the edge to a day's sport.

The easiest and best known method of constructing a spoon bait is by using the domestic models; tea, dessert, table and serving spoons. Any tattered old type of spoon will do; in fact the older models have a deeper, better shaped bowl and spin more easily than the modern counterpart. Bright, shiny colours are not essential either, some of our most successful lures having been downright scruffy.

The safest way of preparing a spoon bait is to leave the handle attached, using it to hold the bowl firmly whilst two holes are drilled at its front and rear ends, each about 2–3 mm in size. Then the handle can be cut free with a hacksaw, the cut smoothed off with a file, and a split ring and a treble (in keeping with the size of spoon – rather too large than too small), together with a

102 Construction of a 'copper and silver' from tablespoons.

swivel, can be added at the front and rear end respectively.

Of course, domestic spoons are not the only source of spoon material – old car and motor cycle headlamp reflectors have the right shape and umpteen may be cut from them with a pair of tin snips. Curved pieces of a car bumper make excellent spoons, especially the large ones for deep trolling, although they can be the Devil's own work to cut. The best solution to this problem is to make a template of the required size, draw as many spoon shapes around it that the length of bumper will take, and then get them cut professionally at an engineering works or garage. Yes, there will be a charge for the work – but believe us, to the best of our knowledge, you cannot get extra large spoons anywhere at the moment.

Ultra light spoons can be cut from pieces of alloy or sheet copper. Once cut they must be shaped – and there are two ways of tackling this job. The first method requires a large wooden block, one that is delivered, ready for splitting for use in the domestic fire is ideal. Into this a large spoon shape is either

103 Cut and shaped spoon with component parts ready for assembly.

chiselled or burnt by means of a heated iron constantly applied until the required shape is hollowed out. When this former is made, it is a simple matter to lay the metal blank over it, and tap it into the required shape with a hammer (which will give a fair representation of scale pattern) or by using a wooden drift, which will leave a smooth surface when the shape is formed.

The second method is useful only for the smaller spoons, and needs two very large domestic table spoons, complete with

104 Blades for bar spinners which can be purchased from McHardys of Carlisle.

105 First stage in making a spoon bait: marking out from the template.

106 Cutting the spoon: notice that hands are kept well away from metal edges.

107 Beating the shape: the log base has a depression cut into its face, and the ball end of the hammer is used to set the curve of the spoon.

handles. The metal blank is placed between these, the three components are then placed between the jaws of a vice, which is tightened down. In seconds the spoon will be pressed into shape. Actually, this word 'spoon' has become a bit of a misnomer. Many spinners (either in part or whole) are contained in the heading, but they are not necessarily spoon-shaped. Some which spring to mind are the 'Toby' type lure, and the 'Jim Vincent' lures. We dealt with these and a little of their history and construction in *Spinners, Spoons and Wobbled Baits*. They are both elongated out of the normal spoon shape, and have a flare, or off-set to the front or rear.

There is no limit to the imagination when it comes to designing and constructing new spoons. They only need cutting out of sheet metal of one sort or another, and can be tapped into shape on the wooden block, described above. Ken illustrates one of his own in Photo. 103. He has a contact who is a plumber, and he saves some off-cuts of copper piping for him. This particular lure was made from a 6 in. length of 1 in. piping, cut down the middle, beaten flat, and then cut to shape. The beating to obtain the curve took minutes only, and the beaten effect reflects light well when the lure is retrieved.

We have mentioned the use of metal for spoon making, but, of course, there are other materials that can be used. As an instance, the fore-runner of the Jim Vincent spoon was carved from wood by American Indians, and there is no reason why a light, near floating lure could not be made, painted, and used in a like manner today.

Other thoughts centre around sheet plastic, which can be cut, and then moulded or twisted into shape after a suitable heat treatment of boiling water (never a naked flame) has been applied. And, of course, today there are plastic spoons which spin equally as well as their metal counterparts; we mention a use for these later. One of Barrie's most successful 'Veltics' was home-made with a 2 in. plastic blade.

COLORADO SPOONS

These old-fashioned spinners seem to have disappeared from the angling scene, but they are excellent fish getters, and possess the great advantage of being weighted – an asset where deep pits and lakes are being spun over.

In appearance the Colorado is a spoon with two fins at its front end. Our diagram (Fig. N) gives the shape that must be cut out, and a template from card or tin to the size required takes a short time to produce. Select sheet alloy or copper, and outline the template on it, cutting each lure free with tin snips. These blanks are then given the pressed spoon treatment as outlined in our last section – squeezing them into the required shape with the aid of a vice. After this the vanes at the nose are twisted alternately outwards with a pair of pliers. Now a hole 2–3 mm in diameter is drilled at nose and tail, and the bar, which will go through the length of the spoon, prepared.

It is essential that stout wire is used for this bar; soft wire will bend and jam the spinning operation – as often happens, in fact, with commercial models. As mentioned earlier, we use 24–26 gauge stainless steel piano wire, and in one end of a length of this we slide a swivel, and twist an eye over it. A pair of round-nose pliers are an essential for this operation – the eye of the swivel must not be obstructed in any way. The length of wire is now threaded through the hole at the nose end of the blank, and a barrel lead of a length and weight that will both fit the bowl of the spoon and sink the lure rapidly is threaded in place. The end of the wire is passed through the end hole, a treble hook added, and secured with a twist finish.

Finally the body of the spoon can be painted (we favour red on the concave side, including the weight) or polished as the case may be. As already mentioned, some people add a tying of red wool around the treble, probably to represent the tail fin of a roach we suppose. Pretty to look at, but highly conducive to rust formation, if not on the particular treble to which it is attached, then to the other lures in the box in which it will be carried. If you must have an adornment on the treble then try a small piece of very thin, rigid coloured plastic, cut into a triangle or square, and pushed over the barb of one hook only of the three. Just as effective, without harbouring water at the end of the day.

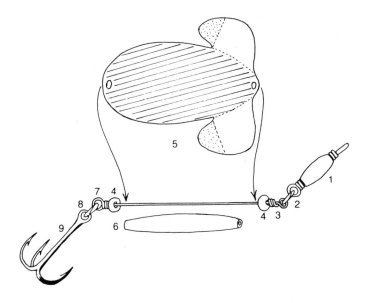

Fig. **N** Colorado spoon or spinner: 1. Swivel; 2. Split ring; 3. Forward loop of axial wire; 4. Bead; 5. Spoon blade outline (shaded area is hammered concave and stippled areas set at opposing angles); 6. Barrel lead for axial wire; 7. Terminal loop of axial wire; 8. Split ring attached to treble hook (9).

THE KIDNEY SPOON

Another golden (though in most cases – silver) oldie that is worth making, especially for use in deep gravel pit pike spinning. Most of the few items we have come across in tackle shops are far too small, so don't be afraid to think big with this one. Use a heavy gauge copper or metal sheet and draw out the kidney shaped vane.

We favour something a good 3 in. long, and once cut, hammer this into a concave shape on the wooden block. Now rig a wire shaft in the same way that we describe for the bar spoon complete with a treble at one end, and load it with a good sized (2 in. at least) barrel lead. Make sure that there is a hole of at least 3 mm drilled in one lobe of the kidney vane, and slide this on the bar, finishing off with the normal swivel and twisted eye. Like the Colorado spoon this is normally painted red on the

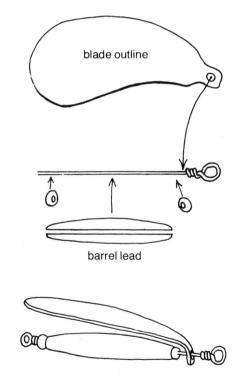

Fig. **O** Kidney (bar) spoon: similar construction to Colorado (Fig. **N**).

inside (concave) part of the blade, with the body painted a like colour – although Ken has had some success with a yellow painted lead.

BAR SPOONS

As the name suggests, a bar spoon consists of a piece of metal, fixed at one or both ends, which can revolve around a central bar that carries both hook and mounting swivel. This central bar may, if required, be loaded with lead or brass, usually taking the form of beading, and mounted to represent the 'body' of a fish. By far the greatest number of spinners in use fall into the first definition we have outlined, i.e. with the blade, vane or spinner mounted at one end only on the central bar.

From the beginning we would commend to the home tackle-maker the excellent kits and various parts offered for sale by many tackle dealers. We illustrate two sets of parts in the book, and it can be seen that there is literally nothing that cannot be produced in the way of spinners from these items – in fact the chance to experiment and design a spinner of one's own using various combinations of the parts is, in itself, a fascinating study.

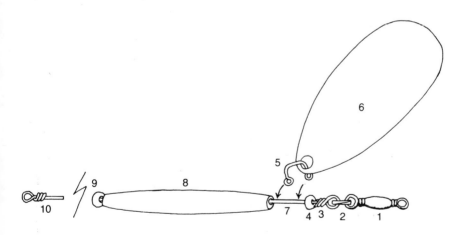

Fig. **P** Bar spoon, basic assembly: 1. Swivel; 2. Split ring; 3. Forward loop of axial wire; 4. Bead; 5. Device for attaching blade (6) to axial wire (7); 8. Barrel lead; 9. Bead; 10. Terminal loop of axial wire.

The parts are not expensive, and some, if not all of them can be utilised with those parts that the angler can produce with ease to help make the complete spinner. We shall see, as we describe in detail the making of a bar type spinner, exactly what these items are.

Blades are the easiest part to manufacture – sheet metal of any sort, old tin, plastic; anything, in fact, can be cut into shape. At the base of each leaf or blade a hole 2 mm in diameter should be drilled a short distance in from the lip. Patterned effects can be made on the blades by crimping with tin snips, beating with a ball hammer, or stamping with a suitable punch. Once the blades are made, they can be painted if this is desired.

The next requirement is a wire shaft on which a body can be formed. Take a 4 in. length of piano wire, 22–24 gauge, and fit on one end a treble. Now bend the wire round to secure it, either with a pair of round-nose pliers, or by using a former. We use a headless 4 in. nail hammered into the end of the bench. Around this the wire (with treble in position) is bent, and twisted on itself with a pair of pliers. It can then be lifted free, the loose end being snipped off.

Next, body material is slid down the shaft. This can be the professionally drilled brass weight, purchased from a tackle shop, or an appropriate size of barrel or round bored bullet – even large coloured beads if a lightweight spinner is required. Leave plenty of wire free – there are still two items to be mounted.

One of these will be the clevice. This is a curved wire loop, to which the blade fits, and which in turn fits on the shaft of the body. These fiddly little pieces are the devil to bend and twist out of fine, stiff wire (the shape required is self-explanatory from the diagram) and this is one of the items we would mention as being well worthy of purchase from a dealer.

Set the vane into the clevice, slide it on the shaft, and then attach a swivel by the same method as described for the treble. Although the job is then, to all intents and purposes, complete, we suggest that if any form of lead or corrosive metal has been used for weights on the body that they should either be painted, or coated in clear varnish.

THE ODDS AND ENDS

Quite frankly one could write a complete book of ideas and suggestions in this section – especially on new spinners and materials for them. But we must first content ourselves with describing an old favourite.

The Mackerel spinner should, by rights, come under the heading of sea fishing lures, but because of our own (and other anglers) success with it, we decided to include it here. The cost of a finished lure is little in the shop, and this naturally tends to constant usage and loss. But they can be very cheaply prepared by cutting the blade to the shape shown in diagram (Fig. Q) from an old tin box – tobacco-tin lids are ideal.

To this body is soldered a length of thin copper piping (your local model shop is the ideal place to find this) equal in length to the blade itself. Now a wire shaft with treble is prepared (see bar-spoon construction) and to this is added a small coloured bead before being threaded through the piping itself, ensuring a smooth surface against which the lure can turn. Finally, the eye swivel is added, the wire being turned back on itself with the customary twist finish.

So far, we have only considered blades as spinning objects. There are excellent lures though, that can be made using small

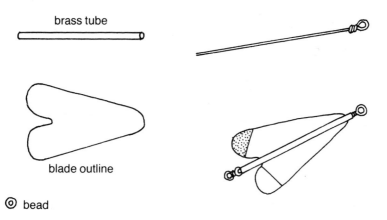

brass tube

blade outline

◎ bead

Fig. **Q** Mackerel spinner: brass tube must be glued or brazed to the blade; wings of blade (one stippled) set at opposing angles.

108 Various 'flies-cum-lures' tied by Ken Whitehead.

propellers. Ken got the idea of using them following an hour or two's browsing through one of the old-time fishing catalogues. In the Salmon Fly section he noticed several large flies – resembling small fish more than any fly in fact – that had a small propeller mounted at the nose. The implications of this were obvious – during the retrieve it would have an audible appeal (via the vibration through the water), quite apart from its visible effect through colour and shape.

Practically any fly can be made with this attachment, providing that the hook and body construction are large enough to support the blade, which must, if it is to be effective, be reasonably large itself. Ken started with a Jersey Herd, has success with this, and discussed the result with Dennis Howell, the pro-fly-tyer at Don's fishing tackle shop in Edmonton. He promptly sat down and tied up a roach imitation with blades added, and this was featured in our book on *Spinners, Spoons and Wobbled Baits*.

The spinning blades themselves? Well, these miniature propellers can be cut from very thin tin, and then the blades can be bent in opposite directions to obtain the necessary bite in the water. But an easier answer is to purchase them ready-made – a matter of pence each – and we found a supply of them listed in McHardys of Carlisle's tackle catalogue.

Naturally, a dozen variations of this last fly/spinner scheme immediately present themselves – tube flies with spinning blades (à la bar spoon) or propellers; fly bodies with small bar spoons; a Devon Minnow body with . . . well, the permutations for new spinners both small and large are legion. Try them all in the rough state at first, then concentrate on producing a polished and well balanced final item. Above all – don't give up if your results look a little bit on the 'amateur' side. Take it from us – the fish most certainly will not tell the difference.

PLUG BAITS

Our book *Plugs and Plug fishing* dealt pretty thoroughly with the making of plugs themselves and we make no apology for presenting now, as we did then, a quick breakdown on the various types of plug that are in use, their performance and construction, before we look into the D.I.Y. aspects.

There are four main categories of plugs. First are the surface lures, working on, or at the most within an inch or so of the surface itself. They have a square nose as a rule, are made from light material that will float, and are designed to be jerked, or 'popped' back to the angler over the surface, rather in the manner of a struggling large insect or small animal. A variation on the usual squat nosed plug is the torpedo shape with propeller blades mounted on the nose, or nose and tail end, which are designed to revolve and thrash along the surface during a retrieve.

Floating/diving lures have an angled step, or protruding vane set at the nose which will drive the plug into a shallow dive during a retrieve – the depth and rate of dive depending on the size of vane at the model's head and, of course, the rate at which it is drawn through the water. When not being worked by the angler, floating/diving lures rise and sit on the surface.

109 Some of Barrie's home-made plugs.

Sinking plugs are manufactured from heavy material, or buoyant material that has been weighted to ensure the lure's slow drop from the surface to the bottom after the cast has been made. There may be a small vane at the lure's head, assisting the lure deep down whilst it is on the move, but by and large they are made to look like fish without any artificial adornments (other than hooks, of course).

Deep diving plugs are among the most interesting that the angler can produce. They have the normal tapered-type body, but at the nose end the plug is fitted with a king-sized metal or plastic vane. The effect of water pressing against this during the retrieve is to make the lure run deep, and hold down close to the bottom all the time that the re-wind is kept up.

Now, from this very potted synopsis we can make a list of interesting points worth remembering during the construction of plugs in general. A straight, squat, or obverse finish to the nose end of a plug will keep it on the surface – as well as the true cigar shape, without any diving adornments. Plugs finished with a nose at right-angles to the water's surface, or those fitted with a protruding vane will dive on the retrieve, the amount of dive largely dependent on the size (or weight) and angle of the vane. And finally the obvious fact that if you want to make a sinking plug that will sink on its own volition, then you must construct it, or adapt it from a suitable material.

One or two other odd facts are worth remembering. The shape of the plug's body (within reason) is probably immaterial to its performance or attraction, and basically the number of joints that the plug possesses can be unlimited – we show one in *Plugs and Plug Fishing* which has six segments.

Now to materials which can be used in plug making – and this includes all the odds and ends that may be necessary, not just those for making the bodies. Wood, naturally, comes to mind as the best choice, and dowel of various lengths and circumferences are a must. Try to get timber with the closest grain possible, and store flat until required for use, otherwise a 'set' will soon take place.

Of course, there are always broom handles, and some old, excellent hard lengths of timber can be obtained by keeping one's eyes open for them. They are difficult to work, but provide a very strong body on which the various hooks, swivels, etc. can be firmly attached. Another source of seasoned timber is old walk-

110 Barrie's Waddle-arse plug, ready assembled.

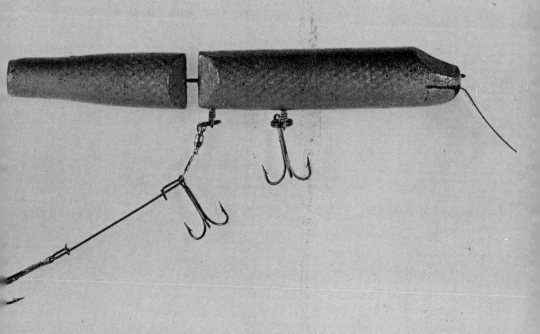

ing sticks and canes, which can be picked up cheaply at most jumble sales and junk shops. Finally, plastic dowel of any sort is worth looking out for, and also odd squares or oblong pieces in any colour.

Hooks, swivels, and cabled Alasticum are necessary, together with sheet metal (of any sort) for use as diving vanes. Last, but not least, there is a use for a few screw-eyes or ring-eyed screws, although we always tend to avoid these wherever possible.

Not surprisingly it is possible to buy most of the things described above in kit form. Messrs McHardys of Carlisle sell various body shapes (see Photo. 111) moulded from first-rate plastic, that only need fitting out with vanes and other accoutrements which McHardys also supply. There are innumerable combinations that can be fitted up with these parts, and the cost reduction per finished lure makes the whole venture worthy of consideration.

111 Plastic plug bodies from McHardys of Carlisle, ready drilled and requiring only hooks and swivels etc.

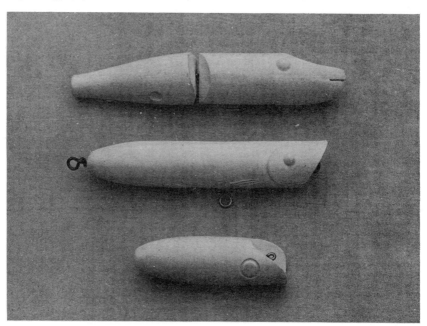

Even if you decide to do the body work yourself then the various fixings that are sold can be a time-saving investment, and for the not-so-skilled angler they will go a long way towards producing a professional looking plug.

Now for a blow-by-blow account of plug making, using either wood or plastic for the body. We find it easiest to make several plug bodies in one session, even though we only need one or two for the tackle box at that particular time. The extra shaped but unrigged blanks can be kept in reserve, and by working to this method we avoid constant shifting of tools as each stage is finished.

Taking a suitable length of dowel, measure off several lengths into the size required, mark, and then clamp the dowel end-up in a vice. In this position it is the work of minutes to shape the end into a point or cigar-stub end with a Surform and wood file. Once shaped, the plug is cut free with a straight saw cut across, so that the next length will be ready for cutting out. If it is neces-

112 Simple shallow and deep-diving one-piece plugs ready for the painting stage.

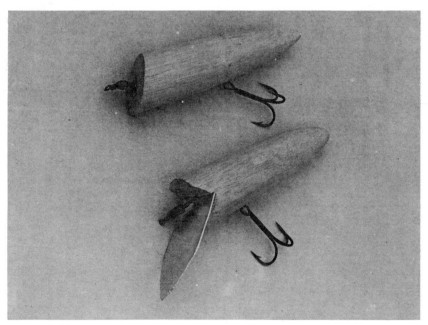

sary for the plug to have an angled face, or a V-slot, it should be cut when it is free of the parent piece itself, taking care to wrap the plug body in cloth or rolled cardboard so that no vice marks are cut into its side.

Diving vanes should be outlined on a sheet of alloy or copper, cut out, and mounted on the nose by small screws and Araldite glue. It is also possible to hold the vane in place by using a screw-eye through the vane and into the wood itself, spreading Araldite under the vane and along the threads of the screw before tightening down. But this is a rather haphazard method of mounting, especially for either nose swivels or hooks.

The only successful and sure way of fixing anything to a plug is by drilling holes through the plug body itself, then threading this hole with cabled Alasticum and attaching trebles, swivels, etc. to it (see Fig. **R**). This hole boring is probably the most difficult thing in plug making. Use the longest drill bit available, and once the hole is made, pass a length of red-hot wire through it to ensure that there are no splinters that can cause hang-ups as the Alasticum is passed into place.

The Waddle Arse plug described by Barrie in *Plugs and Plug Fishing* utilises this technique. The tricky bit is pushing the swivels into the holes made on the ventral side of each plug part. Begin by preparing an eye (as described in the above sections)

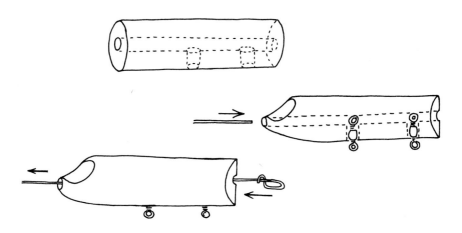

Fig. **R** Waddle-arse plug construction. See Photo. 110.

113 Wire work: Barrie is twisting an eye in steel wire, using a headless nail for a former.

on one end of the piano wire. Then, using a length of wire several inches too long, push the end opposite the eye into the plug body so that it passes through the eye of the swivel which has been located in the ventral hole. The problem is that the eye of the swivel turns as you push it into the hole so that you may need a thin bladed knife or a sliver of celluloid to hold the eye at right-angles to the long hole through the plug body. This is the only difficult part, and the rest can be put together as is apparent from the diagram.

Sinking plugs are difficult to produce unless one is able to get hold of high-density material from which to make the bodies – i.e. plastic of any sort. It is all a question of casting around for short scrap lengths of suitable material; no easy job, but not impossible by any means. Ken had some success in finding an old bedside lamp, and he utilised the plastic that formed the support

241

for several bodies. Failing plastic, then wood must be used and weighted, by drilling holes along the belly of the lure into which lead in the form of shot or bullets can be fitted and glued, any gaps being filled in by the use of plastic wood.

Not all plug bodies are round. There are the banana-shaped bodies that can be quite effective and these can often be copied by using brush handles, old toothbrush types heated in boiling water and bent into a curved shape, the head being cut free, and both ends drilled. Suitable hooks and swivels can be mounted and the job is done.

We mentioned an odd surface lure at the beginning of this section. The cigar-shaped body with propellers at nose and/or tail is simple to produce, and highly effective in use. We have also discovered that when these propellers (cut from sheet alloy and bent into shape) are mounted on a sinking or weighted body they also make excellent mid-water lures. The propellers need not be in proportion to the body – oversized and brightly painted blades are successful, providing that they spin freely.

Always on the look-out for new plug bodies, we are at the moment experimenting with latex, which can be moulded into various shapes. We were prompted in this by the fly fishermen who have been using the material to form the body of flies, and more especially nymphs. Briefly, Copydex or Caratex latex adhesives are smeared on a sheet of glass (using a finger) into strips as wide as necessary, the width, naturally, governing the length of the lure and each strip six or more inches long. Don't try to spread the latex too far though, otherwise the body will be far too thin. In an hour or so the latex will have dried off and can then be rolled into a sausage, which forms a body. Two or three strips can be rolled one on the other, until a reasonable thickness is formed; sufficient for a small plug shape.

Now, the problems in this experimental process are innumerable – and so far unresolved. For instance, we are not sure yet how 'tooth-resistant' the latex will prove to be after a tussle with a hooked fish, or even how long the body will last in the water with use – regardless of any varnish that can be applied. Also, a very great deal of the stuff is required to produce a single body of small size. We have tried using a thin brass tube as a former, and have wound the latex round this to develop the shape, but that is as far as we have got at the moment. Even if

114 Barrie's workbench, showing some of the tools and materials used in making spinning lures.

we are unable to turn the stuff into large enough bodies to rig out a plug, then we feel sure that they will be first-rate bodies for 'poppers'.

Poppers are a popular lure in the United States, and equally good for chub, perch, etc. over here. Fig. S shows how they are constructed – using a long shanked hook that acts as the body chassis, the body is shaped, and then mounted to it. If only we can find a sufficiently affluent sponsor to supply our needs we feel sure that wine bottle corks, carefully extracted and with the ends filed and cut into shape, are ideal for the job. Failing this (and hang the expense) we must buy some new corks so conveniently provided with the increasingly popular D.I.Y. brewing kits. Incidentally, if you are going to cut cork, use a sharp knife repeatedly moistened by dipping the blade into cold water. This helps overcome resistance and gives the blade more control during the slicing process.

243

Once shaped, a hole can be pierced along the length of the cork, and the shank of the hook pushed through it, after a thorough smearing with Araldite. Make sure that the eye of the hook is clear of glue, and the job is done. Slow sinking poppers can be made by the same method, but before offering up the shank of the hook through the body, wrap a few turns of lead wire around it. Naturally, the hole through the body should be slightly larger than normal, but not so big that there is any risk of it parting company with the hook.

The make and break point on a plug – the thing that decides whether the lure looks the work of a rank amateur, or a possible professional item – is in the painting. There can be no mass production method in this; each item will need time and effort spent on it and the more expended, the better and longer lasting the results. Start by sealing the grain of all wood or cork bodies with an undercoating of paint or sanding sealer, and allow plenty of time for this to dry. Then, decide on the pattern that will be painted. Single coloured plugs are simple enough but those with dual colours, corresponding to the mid-line division that is normally found on a real fish, need some careful lining out if colours are to be prevented from running one into the other.

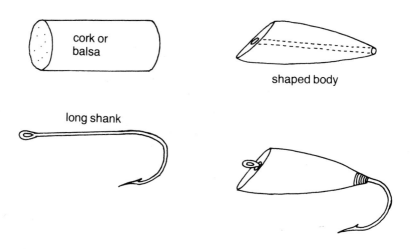

Fig. S Basic surface popper construction: hook should be glued in position and bound as shown.

A strip of sellotape along each side of the body will keep a crisp, straight line between the colours – we described the method when we discussed painting wooden or plastic Devon Minnows. A trick worth remembering is that by using a piece of perforated zinc as a template and spraying over it, it is possible to make a fairly good imitation of a scale finish.

Whatever method you use, do, please, keep your colours natural. Yes, there are stacks of reds, whites, yellows and blues in the professionally produced model – but we are firmly convinced that these colours catch more fishermen than fish. Keep 'em natural, using bars of yellow, or a scale finish – and finally, use a good coating of clear varnish over the whole body to help reduce scratch damage.

DEADBAIT SPINNING RIGS

In this section dealing with the use of deadbaits, we are referring to pure spinning rigs only, where the bait is made to perform a complete revolution in flight. Wobbled baits do not require a vane to set them in motion; their wobbling action is obtained from the curve set into the bait's body when it is mounted on to the hooks of the rig. In fact, most deadbait mounts make good wobbling flights once the bait is set into them with a good curve turned into the tail end.

To make a small fish revolve requires some careful work on the part of the angler in producing and adjusting a set of vanes that will be set at the head of the bait. These can be manufactured from sheet perspex or thin sheet metal, and in Fig. T we show a diagram of a deadbait spinning rig suitable for sprats or small roach and dace. It is remarkably efficient in use, and costs literally pence to make.

Start by cutting the spinning vanes to the shape shown in the diagram. A pair of sharp scissors will do the work in seconds – and aim to cut the shape rather on the big side, so that any trimming or adjusting to the rate of spin can be done later. If the first two or three sets of vanes that you cut out vary considerably in size, it is worth making a template in metal which can be drawn round and will ensure uniformity.

Now take a length of medium/thin copper wire (fine gauge piano wire is also excellent) and cut off a 7 in. piece. Bend the last 2 in. of this into a U-shape, and slide a swivel into the bend. Next, offer up the spinning vane into the 'U' as shown in the diagram with the sharp end of the vane pointing forward. Bend the short end of wire down over the back of the vane, and twist it firmly round the larger end, securing both vane and swivel firmly in place. Snip off any unwanted wire at the short end when three or four turns have been made, and bend the remaining length of wire straight.

The body pin (which is what the long end of wire left will be) must now be cut back until it is three or four inches long, and the end sharpened into a point. Heat some water, and when boiling dip the vanes into it and leave them until the plastic becomes soft. Bend them both outwards with a pair of pliers in opposing directions, then put them under the cold tap and run water on them to cool and harden them off again.

If weight is to be added to the flight (to assist in casting) it can be fixed to the body pin behind the spinning vane either by means of lead wire bound round the pin and secured with a coating of Araldite glue, or by means of a barrel lead of an appropriate size and weight slid up on the pin, and glued into place.

Take a small, fine wire split ring and secure it into the eye of the swivel through which the wire of the pin is running. Cut a 5 in. length of medium strength Alasticum cable, and mount two trebles on it in the same way that we described in the section on deadbait rigs. This cable is then passed through the split ring, turned back on itself and secured by a series of firm twists. Cut off the surplus wire, Araldite the joint, and the job is done.

In use, the wire pin and weight are pushed down into the mouth and throat of the bait, and one or both trebles are pushed into its flanks to hold it in place. An extra precaution, where long distance casting is going to be practised, is to bind the bait with a number of turns from a length of fine nylon or white sewing silk, around body and trace. This is especially desirable where sprats are used as bait – they are usually soft, and break up easily.

Like all things, practice makes perfect in this sort of work. Start by making one or two big spinning flights, and in a short

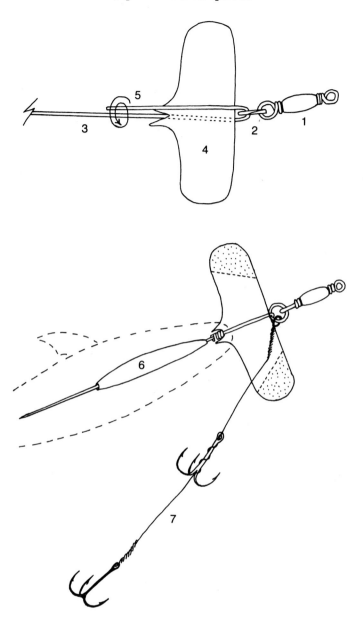

Fig. **T** Sprat spinner (=deadbait spinner) rig: 1. Swivel; 2. Split ring; 3. Spike wire; 4. Blade; 5. Part of spike wire bent back for twisting to hold blade tightly; 6. Barrel lead *glued* in position; 7. Wire and *fixed* trebles for placing on side of bait, position of which is shown by broken lines.

time one's fingers will become dexterous enough to scale down the operation until mounts capable of holding a large minnow can be made. Several anglers have watched us when spinning, and on examining the mount, have remarked on its apparent flimsy construction. This is not the case; the strength of the tackle lies through the split ring and treble mount. The spinning vanes and body pin play no part in hooking and landing a fish.

We discussed scaling-down the operation – but, of course, it is possible to go the other way, and scale up production until one has produced a tackle large enough to support the spinning of a small herring. Where this is attempted, it is wise to use two lengths of Alasticum with mounted hooks, so that both flanks of the bait can be secured.

Bibliography

The following list is far from exhaustive in the field of D.I.Y. tackle making, but it is intended to help the angler extend his expertise along certain lines not covered in this volume, as for example in *detailed* fly tying: we covered the fundamental steps and basic examples. Some of the books are out of print, but may still be in local libraries. Others may need reference to a copyright library. Those marked with an asterisk contain tackle making tips but are not primarily about tackle making.

Bartles, B., *Match Fishing Tackle and Baits*, A. & C. Black, 1975.

Buller, F. & Falkus, H., *Falkus and Buller's Freshwater Fishing*, Macdonald & Jane's, 1975.

Civardi, A. & Rashbrook, F. *The Know How Book of Fishing*. Usborne Publishing Ltd, 1976.

Fisherman's Handbook Advanced Guide, Marshall Cavendish Partworks Ltd, 1978–9.

George, M., In *Angling Times*, EMAP National Publications Ltd, 1978–9.

Goddard, J., *Trout Flies of Stillwater*, A. & C. Black, 1979 (4th ed.).

*Housby, T. & Linsell, K., *Coarse Fishing Illustrated*, Barrie & Jenkins, 1966.

Ingham, M. & Walker, R., *Drop Me A Line*, Macgibbon and Kee, 1964.

*Lane, B., *Float Fishing*, Cassell, 1976.

Lane, B. & Graham, C., *Billy Lane's Encyclopaedia of Float Fishing*, Pelham Books, 1971.

*Marshall-Hardy, E., (revised ed. L. Cacutt), *Angling Ways*, Barrie & Jenkins, 1973.

Pryce-Tannatt, T. E., *How to Dress Salmon Flies*, A. & C. Black, 1977 (new edition).

Rice, F., *Fly-Tying Illustrated*, David & Charles, 1976.

Stewart, T., *Fifty Popular Flies*, vols. 1–4, Ernest Benn Ltd, 1962–73.

Sugg, R., Whitehead, K. & Vare, A., *Fly Tying*, Rod & Gun Publishing, 1973.

Townsend, D. C., *Game Fishing Devices*, A. & C. Black, 1979.

Veniard, J., *Fly Dressers' Guide*, A. & C. Black, 1970 (4th ed.).

Vincent, S-J., *The Artificial Fly*, A. & C. Black, 1979.

Walker, R., *Rod Building for Amateurs*, An Angling Times Book.

*Walker, R., *Still-Water Angling*, David & Charles, 1975 (revised 4th ed.).

*Wheat, P., *The Observer's Book of Coarse Fishing*, Frederick Warne & Co. Ltd, 1976.

Whitehead, K. & Vare, A., *Knots for the Angler*, Camden, 1975 (revised ed.).

Whitehead, K. & Vare, A., *Rod Building*, Rod and Gun Publishing, 1975.

Index

251